More Than Just Ore

The Era that Really Made Ely

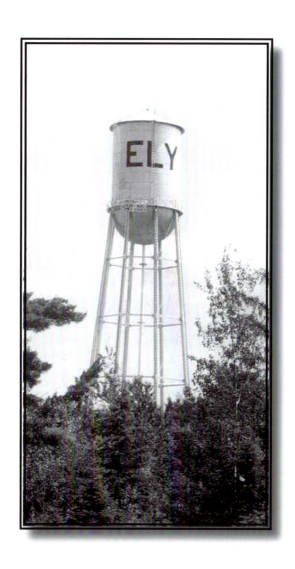

MORE THAN JUST ORE
The Era that Really Made Ely

ISBN: 978-0-9890478-2-1

Dovetailed Press LLC

Book design and publication assistance by
Marlene Wisuri
Dovetailed Press LLC

Printed and bound in the
United States of America

Published by
Ely-Winton Historical Society
1900 E Camp St,
Ely, MN 55731
(218) 365-3226
www.vcc.edu/ewhs

*Ely seen from the ski jump once located on the northwest part of town, one can see the
high school (1924), along with the Old High (1905), and Washington Elementary (1915).*

DEDICATION

To All Those Whose Lives Were Punctuated
Every Eight Hours by the Mine Whistles

ACKNOWLEDGEMENTS

Many ideas and much research go into the making of any book. In this case, the Ely-Winton Historical Society and its extensive archive of local pictures is to be particularly cited. These pictures form the core of this book. The Brownell historical picture collection may be better known, but the historical society's own and even larger archive was my real inspiration. It has become especially valuable since it continues Ely's pictorial history where the Brownell collection ended. These archives are a lasting tribute to the residents of Ely—they and their families have graciously donated or shared literally thousands of pictures that preserve another era of our history. However, it should be noted that the pictures that were used were only ones that the historical society has in its possession. Pictures of people, events, and buildings were not included if they were not in our collections.

The people who helped grow this idea into a book comprise a "village." Those who contributed to this book in quite different ways include Nan and Gerry Snyder, the Rayman family in memory of Tom Rayman, Women's Life Insurance Society, Margaret Sweet, Anne Stewart, Judy Swenson, Ken Hupila, Pat Koski, Sally Fauchald, Judy Horns, Jim Klobuchar, Michael Hillman, Louis Bernard, Leonard Koponen, Molly Pratt, the Ely Chamber of Commerce, the W A Fisher Co., and the editor/publisher Marlene Wisuri. Without their vision, gracious help, and encouragement this part of Ely's history would have remained in file folders and boxes.

David Kess   2014

TABLE OF CONTENTS

◆ ◆ ◆

"...It was a country that demanded and abused, inspired and rewarded. It did all of those things to the immigrants I remember. But before they worked their last they engraved for us a truth: that much of this country's greatness springs from the struggles of its people, the ones it first exploited, and then needed."

"The Red Dirt Ennobled Their Faces"
Eight Miles Without a Pothole
Jim Klobuchar
October 25, 1984

FROM THE BEGINNING

The story of each of Minnesota's several dozen Iron Range mining towns is rather unique. Ely differs from the others mostly because of its geographical location. It is often referred to as being "at the end of the road." And so it is—bordering the million acre Boundary Waters Canoe Area and set in the midst of lakes and forests. This setting has influenced the lives of its settlers and their offspring. The younger generation often left the area soon after being schooled here. Many frequently return for visits with some deciding to retire here.

The lakes and the woods seem to call them back, but so does the quality of life: plucky but friendly people, a casual social atmosphere, attractive lakeshore properties, public services, and a lively arts community.

The early prospectors, settlers, and immigrants however came to a harsh gray world: raw wilderness, no organized town or government, makeshift dwellings, a cold climate, and often dangerous work. A town did evolve—electricity and other amenities came about, law and order were established, and the unions brought about safer and better working conditions in the mines. Iron ore worth millions was mined. Good schools sent well prepared students to colleges and universities, even to places such as Harvard and West Point. While few immigrants had expected educational opportunities for themselves, they did see their dreams fulfilled in the nearly unlimited ones open to their children. Their world was a fresh green one.

Those who lived, worked, played, and stayed here during the "mining era" forged another culture beyond the one they brought from the "old country." They learned readily from their neighbors: the Finns, Swedes, Yugoslavs, Cornish "Cousin Jacks," and Scotch-Irish. Men worked side by side with one another in the mines. A number went together to night school and most became American citizens. Some intermarried, marched in parades together, and joined fraternal organizations and churches. They often learned some of each others' native tongues. Ethnic prejudice and class distinction never completely disappeared, but a sense of equality and neighborliness did evolve. In that way the town really reinvented itself.

The pages of the book that follows showcase pictures from the daily lives of people in Ely from 1887 – 1967. The sobering appendix brings to light meticulously researched statistics for mining casualties during the eighty years of underground mining. The outlook for the families affected by these tragedies was truly a dark and uncertain one.

This book should not be looked upon as a history of the mining operations. Instead, it focuses on the sociology of the people who lived, worked, and died here during that era. The pictures highlight their common joys, sorrows, and achievements as families. Here is to be found a glimpse back at their weddings, funerals, organizations, parades, protests, and picnics.

For over the fifty years past and former residents have donated more than 15,500 photographs to the Ely-Winton Historical Society. Those selected for this book will give the reader a new perspective into this vibrant era.

Note: The Brownell picture collection is so named for Lee Brownell (1909-1987). He first began collecting old pictures when as a child he came across several boxes of them in his grandmother's shed. As word of his interest spread around town, his collection grew to approximately 3000 pictures. It dates from the late 1880s to about the 1950s. Mr. Brownell became the de facto historical society before one was formally organized in 1962.

A second larger collection of pictures that now numbers more that 15,000 has been accumulated by the Ely-Winton Historical Society. It might be said that this collection begins about where the Brownell ended, although they overlap. There are duplicates in both collections. Both have been catalogued and digitized by the historical society.

—David Kess

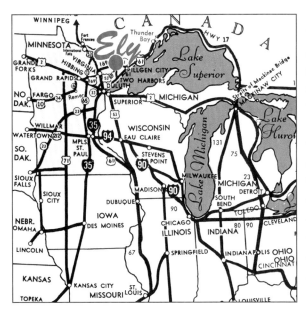

Minnesota sits clearly on the northern tier of states and its location in Minnesota's Arrowhead region shows both its proximity to the Canadian border and its relative remoteness from the rest of the state and the country. It is often identified as a part of the Canadian Shield, or in geological terms within the Duluth Gabbro Complex. *Courtesy of the Ely Chamber of Commerce and the W A Fisher Co., Virginia, MN*

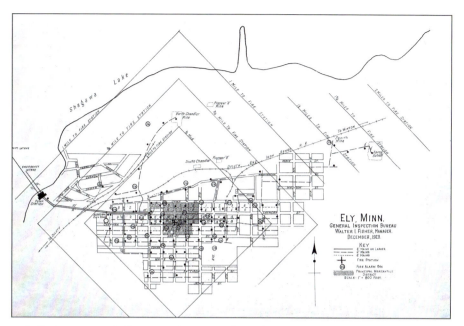

Although it does not delineate the actual outlines, this map from 1923 does indicate where the North and South Chandler Mine shafts are located, as well as those of the Pioneer, Zenith, and Savoy mines. The Sibley had not yet been developed. The south edge of town was a small section of James St. and there is minimal development on the south side of East Sheridan St. The original road to Winton actually went east of Main (not Sheridan) Street. *Courtesy of the Ely-Winton Historical Society*

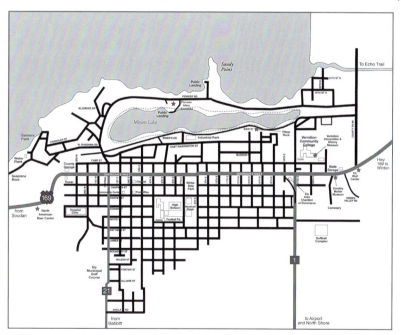

By now many of the underground tunnels in the mines have collapsed and ground water has filled the void creating what is now known as Miner's Lake. The town site has grown south as far as Ahola Road and the area south of East Sheridan St. and east of the school campus has become residential development. Vermilion Community College occupies a space just south and east of the former Zenith and Savoy mines. The road to Winton (State Highway 169) proceeds east from Sheridan St. *Courtesy of the Ely Chamber of Commerce and the W A Fisher Co, Virginia, MN*

THE EARLY YEARS
◆ ◆ ◆

This is perhaps one of the most iconic pictures of Ely. According to legend, two orphaned moose calves were brought into Ed Crossman's tavern. He housed them in a livery thought now to have been on First Avenue and they were eventually trained to pull a sleigh. Mrs. Crossman apparently did well with handling them and is shown here with a friend, Mrs. Adamson. The exact date is unknown, but it is thought to be in the late 1880s or very early 1900s. Ely was a frontier town without any public utilities and few amenities.

View of what was to become downtown Sheridan and Chapman Streets. In the very center is a log building housing Cormack General Merchandise/Chandler House Hotel. It was replaced with a brick building in 1922 which today houses Voltz Technology.

Even back in the early 1900s children found time and places to play games involving a ball. The town was still young—there are wooden sidewalks here on East Harvey Street across from the present Post Office. In the background can be seen the wooden water tower that once stood where the present City Hall is located. The three nearly identical houses in the background are still standing now in 2014, although their appearances have been altered some.

An early view of Ely, probably around 1910, Pioneer Mine Shaft B on the left, the steeples of the First Lutheran Church, St. Anthony's Catholic Church, and Bethany Lutheran Church on the horizon.

The rich ore deposits were of no value without a means of getting them to steel mills for processing. Before there was even a real road to Ely, the railroad was built (1887). It provided the means of transporting ore out and getting supplies and people in, so the local depot was at the very heart of the frontier town.

Engine No. 9 at Ely Station

The very first passenger train out of Ely was on July 4, 1888.

A view of Ely in 1888.

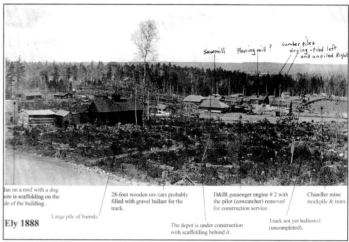

Sawmill   Planing mill ?   Lumber piles drying - Piled left and unpiled Right

Man on a roof with a dog here is scaffolding on the side of the building.

Large pile of barrels

Ely 1888

28-foot wooden ore cars probably filled with gravel ballast for the track.

The depot is under construction with scaffolding behind it.

D&IR passenger engine # 2 with the pilot (cowcatcher) removed for construction service.

Track not yet ballasted (uncompleted).

Chandler mine stockpile & tram.

Note the cut over landscape in the background of this very early picture of two Ely ladies, Mrs. Chinn and Mrs. McMahon and their children. The land appears this way no doubt because it will be mined in the near future.

The Vesi (Finnish) Temperance Society built a large hall on Camp St. that was used for dramatic productions, lectures, concerts, weddings, and programs of all sorts. It became known as the Finnish Opera House as small scale operas were also staged there. In later years, as the Temperance Society diminished in numbers, it became a silent movie theater. Vaudeville and other touring groups also appeared here. Eventually a new movie theater was built to accommodate the "talkies" and the building was sold and renovated as a bowling alley. It remains as such today, but ironically also has a bar and lounge.

In 1900 the city was forced to move its burial grounds, which were on private property at the time, to the east side of town. Actually it was almost a mile from the edge of town at the time. The large gathering is of the Scandinavian Fraternity of America (SFA) which existed in Ely from 1900 to about 1940. There are four new gravesites here, one being a Jacobson and the other appearing to be a Carlson. The lapel ribbons are for members of the lodge. Just to the right of the large cross on the horizon one can see "Old High" and the Catholic church further to the right. The land is quite bare of trees, no doubt mainly a result of the clear-cutting. Some of the land would be for pastures and other of it for gardens or farming.

Catholic funeral procession on Camp St. in 1900. The church is in the upper left and the Methodist is to its right in the picture. Notice the brass band, the unpaved streets, and the horse-drawn wagon. The priest in the wagon is Fr. Andrew Smrekar. Many of the small frame houses are still standing but have been remodeled and added onto. The picket fences were there not for decoration but to keep wandering animals, such as cows, out of the garden.

The Sampo Brass Band was under the direction of Charles Kleemola. It was comprised largely of Finns and was one of the first of its kind in the state. Mr. Kleemola achieved some renown with the publishing of his marching music.

Although this photo of an early band under the direction of Mr. John Kinsman is labeled as Ely's first city band, more often credit for the first city band is given to the Sampo Band.

A gathering of a number of Slovenian families at the Muhvich home on 5th Avenue East and Sheridan Street, all here for the Fourth of July, 1898. Included are such familiar Ely names as Matesha, Muhvich, Sturk, Lobe, and Weinzierl (who were German). Some were from Calumet and Tower. Just to the right is Joe Rupert, a volunteer in the Spanish-American War.

Only a few years after mining operations began and the town emerging, Sandy Point was already the scene of many recreational activities. This shows boat racing on the lake off Sandy Point in July of 1893. It would appear that the opposite shoreline had not yet been logged off.

Sandy Point was a picturesque spot on Shagawa Lake directly across the road from the road on the north side of the underground mines. The land was owned by the mining company and developed as a recreational area for use by company officials, employees, and the townspeople. It had a perfect swimming area with a sandy beach. The picture shows a school picnic there in 1909. As the pavilion and docks began to age and need extensive repairs, the mining company closed the area to the public in the 1930s and the city developed land further west into what became known as Semer's Park. John Semer had donated the land for use as a city park in 1916 but it was not developed until the Works Progress Administration (WPA) stepped into the picture to make it useable.

These ladies and gentlemen look to be out on a boating excursion on one of the area lakes. This would have been in the very early 1900s or possibly even earlier.

Dr. Shipman, Ely's first resident physician, is shown with his wife Rozella and an unidentified woman posed by a teepee frame. The Shipmans had a summer home on Shagawa lake, as did a number of Indians, but the connection between the two is not apparent. Dr. Shipman's summer home was moved across the ice one winter to a location at 26 East White Street. It is constructed of hand hewn logs which are still visible today.

Fishing was a popular pass time even before there was an official Ely. This included winter ice fishing and on-the-lake summer fishing. Mike Wein-zierl, a local dry goods merchant, is shown here with his impressive catch of fish: however, he doesn't have his fishing rod but his hunting rifle.

Boy and bear from around 1900.

While these three people are presumably a father, son, and daughter, it is the picket fence that speaks of Ely. The fences protected gardens from roaming cows and other "critters."

Despite the absence of polar fleece, mukluks, and Spandex, ladies still enjoyed the winter weather. Shown here on the far left with her heavy woolen coat, hat, skirts and snowshoes is Mrs. A. O. (Josephine) Mills with her friends. She was the daughter of Judge Van Blarcom, a prominent Ely pioneer.

This picture from the early 1900s shows three children in the attire of the day. They could well be from the Chinn family who lived on the 200 block of East Harvey Street, across from where the present Post Office is. The chimneys and rooflines in the background would seem to indicate that these are the three nearly identical houses built by Grant McMahan at the time. Mr. Chinn was a mining captain. The nature of the wooden "structure" near the children is not known.

Studio pictures may have had formal backdrops and subjects were often in their "Sunday best" but there were all sorts of other reasons to have a picture taken of friends even in work day attire. These men are Swedes and Finns from the early 1900s.

When a woman had some money of her own to spend, the place in town to go was to the millinery shop to buy a new hat. The bigger the better. These two ladies remain nameless, as do so many others in the collections of the Ely-Winton Historical Society.

An early Ely family out on a summer outing.

These children and their wagon are pictured in the front yard of the Williams/Oppel house on East Harvey St. Mrs. Williams was Capt. Chinn's daughter. Her daughter Marcella Oppel later lived in the house until she was 100 years old. She lived until the age of 106, spending the last six in the local nursing home. It is not known whether she is one of the children in the picture. Note the steel wheels on the wagon.

Although it is not certain, but knowing that these people's faces and dress resemble other Finnish immigrant families, it is most probably that they too are Finnish and that this family portrait is from the early 1900s.

Back in the days before homes had indoor plumbing, babies were bathed in whatever size container would do the job. This baby obviously is enjoying a warm bath. Adults had larger size tin bathtubs that were set in the middle of the kitchen, near the wood burning cookstove where water was heated. And of course for the Finnish people, the sauna was the way to take a bath.

Growing up in Ely, despite the lack of amenities that we now enjoy, had its very happy moments. Children, then as now, were the future, but parents back then, even with as little as many of them had starting out, saw opportunities for their children that they never dared to think of for themselves. This picture seems to say it all in what people back then saw coming down the road.

MINING THE ORE
◈ ◈ ◈

The Red Dirt Ennobled Their Faces

...When poets celebrated the dignity of man, they might not have been thinking very hard about underground miners. Their faces were smudged from rubbing the rock wall when they set a drill bit or a dynamite stick. The seams in their faces were streaked with ore dirt. They had the caricature look of actors painted by a deranged makeup artist who ignored the rims of white skin under their mining helmets and lathered the rest in red.

From *Eight Miles Without a Pothole*, by Jim Klobuchar
October 25, 1984

These miners from the early days of the Pioneer Mine. The shaft house in the background was constructed then of wood, but later ones were of steel and sheet metal. Candles on their helmets lit the way for the miners.
Courtesy of Isabel Koski from Walter Koski collection

The iron ore deposits near Sandy Point on Shagawa Lake were first discovered by George Stuntz in 1882. Because of the somewhat problematic structure of the ore, the fee holders (investors) who became interested in extracting these deposits looked to existing mining operations in the UK. Mining captains and miners were recruited particularly from Cornwall and were nicknamed "Cousin Jacks." Mining the red rock was always dangerous because of the nature of the surrounding rock formations. The first ore, from the Chandler, was shipped out in 1888 after the railroad had been extended to Ely.

Ore was discovered on the Mesabi Range in the early 1890s. Mining this ore was done by means of open pits (strip mining) using power shovels. The process was both less expensive and labor intensive. After the recession of 1893, mining operations in Ely nearly came to a halt.

The Chandler South Mine was the first mine in Ely, shipping its first ore out by rail in 1888. It was first operated as an open pit mine since the ore body was close to the surface but the mining later was done by tunneling into the sides of the open pit and subsequently then by means of underground mining. Shown above are two early views of the Chandler Mine. The lower photo shows mining apparatus, including a sheave wheel, that were being assembled for the Chandler Mine in 1888.

The man who became the first superintendent of Ely's first mine, the Chandler, was John Pengilly—in the center marked #1. He first came to Ely by canoe, landing on Sandy Point. Within two years he also became the Village of Ely's first president.

Men such as R. B. Whiteside, William Pattison, Martin Pattison, and Dr. W. J. Conan owned the first mining companies. They later were absorbed by the likes of U. S. Steel.

Already in 1906 steel was needed for the structures and equipment used in mining operations. Also because of the relatively unstable nature of the rock and ore deposits in the Ely mines, much timber was required to "shore up" the "ceilings" above the drifts that were being mined. Logging thus supported the mining industry and was an important part of the economy of Ely for many years with the need for timber continuing on until the last year of mining.

Sibley Mine shaft under construction. The Sibley Mine lasted for 55 years, until 1954. It's "glory days" were no doubt during WW II when, like all the mines in Minnesota, ore was being mined to support the massive war effort and its need for trucks, tanks, jeeps, planes, submarines, ships, barges, rifles, helmets, bombs, and artillery of all sorts. Steel was needed for bridges, towers, and railroads. Minnesota miners made a huge "silent" contribution.

Drilling to determine the location and extent of ore deposits was a huge part of mining operations. Shown here is a twelve foot core from the Zenith Mine. The rock formation has the markings of typical pillow lava—the phenomenon that was part of the formation of the ore body.

The following list of names and statistics for Vermilion Range mines was prepared by Dan Hestetune, a retired mining engineer who worked in Ely. The information is taken from the *2010 Skilling's North American Mining Directory*.

Armstrong Bay	1923 to 1923	4,478 tons
Chandler North	1891 to 1942	9.5 million tons
Chandler South	1888 to 1957	2.4 million tons
McComber	1917 to 1918	8,386 tons
Pioneer	1888 to 1967	41.1 million tons
Savoy	1899 to 1916	1.9 million tons
Section 30	1910 to 1923	1.5 million tons
Sibley	1899 to 1954	9.8 million tons
Soudan	1884 to 1963	16 million tons
Zenith	1892 to 1964	21.6 million tons

By 1924 there were at least fifteen abandoned mines. The mines produced tremendous profits for the fee holder (investors). For instance, the Chandler Mine paid stockholders a net profit of $100,000 per month for the first nineteen years of operation.

The largest and longest-lasting of the five Ely mines was the Pioneer Mine. It closed on April Fool's Day, 1967. There were 475 employees when the mine closed. The Pioneer Mine had two operating shaft structures. The "A" shaft still exists on the north side of Miner's Lake and is a part of the Pioneer Mine Heritage complex. This view shows the cant lever that supported the head frame.

The Pioneer "B" shaft stood on the north side of the railroad tracks. The shaft structure was removed following the closing of the mine in 1967 and the railroad bed became the road now known as Miner's Drive.

Mine shafts housed lifts (both cages and skips) that brought miners down into the mine and then back up. The cages carried the miners down into the mine and back up. The skips carried the ore to the surface. The first shafts were constructed of wood but were later replaced by steel structures, such as this one for the Pioneer "A" shaft.

These early miners are posed on and in front of an ore stockpile. The men certainly look serious but are not overly tired looking. There are a few men with pick axes and others with some sticks, which may have been some sort of measuring devices.

The Lucky Boy Mine southwest of the present hospital complex was a relatively short-lived operation. A shaft was sunk and ore removed but records are vague and mostly nonexistent. Gust Johnson is shown at the hoist engine.

This crew of unidentified men who appear to be African-Americans were pictured at another small mine west of Ely near Armstrong Lake. They were likely only there to do initial construction work. The mine was another short-lived one and as unusual as this is, there seems to be little or no information about these men or where they came from.

Shown in the center of this view of the Sibley Mine is the miners' "dry." This was the building used by miners to change into work clothes before a shift and where they showered and put on clean clothing after finishing a shift underground.

The Savoy Mine lasted only until 1916, a mere seventeen years, a bit longer than the Section 30 Mine. It had two mine shafts. This shows Shaft #2.

Although the mine in Section 30 was only a few miles from Ely and was considered part of the Vermilion Range, it mined ore from a deposit somewhat apart from the five Ely mines. Ore was mined for 13 years until 1923.

This shows Zenith miners with hard hats who presumably have just finished a shift or are about to begin one and others in casual clothing who would be off duty. In the foreground is one of several safety awards for having an entire year without a serious accident or fatality.

Working in the early mines was hazardous for a number of reasons. There were few safety standards and no unions to be safeguards for dangerous conditions. Illumination underground at first consisted of candles and carbide lamps. In later years the mine was lit by electric lights and the miners used battery packs to light the lamps on their helmets.

Mining, particularly in the early days, was difficult, dangerous, and back-breaking work. Safety concerns were not seriously addressed until after the unions came into the picture in the 1930s.

Miners at work in the underground tunnels. Notice the railroad rails in both and the prominent timber supports in the one.

The ore deposits were drilled to accept dynamite charges. The ore was thus reduced to smaller sized chunks that could be loaded into the ore cars. These explosions could cause the support timbers to give way or cave-ins to occur. Mudslides were also not uncommon.

There Were Three

Coffee party on an October afternoon,
Six young women at Anna's.
Greetings: "Nice dress," "A new hat?"
Clothing piled on the bed
Embroidered pillow cases.

Smell of dynamite.
Pick and shovel,
Shovel, shovel, shovel.
Mucking ore, one car, two cars.
"You are working too hard Eino."
"I will soon have another mouth to feed."

"Anna is pregnant!"
Motherly advice from a mother of one.
Much teasing, morning sickness,
Marta's new baby, colic and remedies,
"Anna, where is Eino working now?"
"He is working at the Laura."

Sweat, smell of sweat, sweaty back.
Sweaty hair, sweaty face.
Shovel, shovel, shovel.
"What do women talk about, Walter?"
"They are funny. You listen sometime."
"I'll be a good father."
"Timber, bring more timber."
"Lagging."

Warm, moist air smelling of spice cake.
Moisture clinging to windows
Anna's good china - white table cloth.
"Sugar? Cream? More coffee cake?"
New recipes for coffee cake.

"When will the baby come, Eino?"
"I don't know. They come when they are ready."
"More timber. Place the caps."
More lagging.
Three hours to go.

The high cost of sugar.
"The *Daily Worker* says…"
"Eino is making good money now."
"We must go - time to fix supper."
"Goodbye. Take care of yourself, Anna."

Two hours to go.
Last car, make ready for the next shift.
Down the drift, a thud, strange sound.
Rumble, timbers shuddering, red ore from above.
Shifting, caps bending, "Run! Run! Too late!"
Crushing blackness, smothering weight.
Bone's snapping.
"Anna! Our baby! Our baby!"

Lungs filling with red ore.
Breathing ore.
Blackness forever.
No more pain.

Red sunset on a white house.
Red sunset on white curtains, all red.
Party dishes done, supper to make.
"Everyone liked my cookies: Gretta had three."
A wife should look pretty when her husband
comes home.
"Where is Eino?" Waiting, waiting.
"The night seems darker tonight,
"How long just we wait, I and our baby?
"Patience. Waiting seems forever."

Louis Bernard

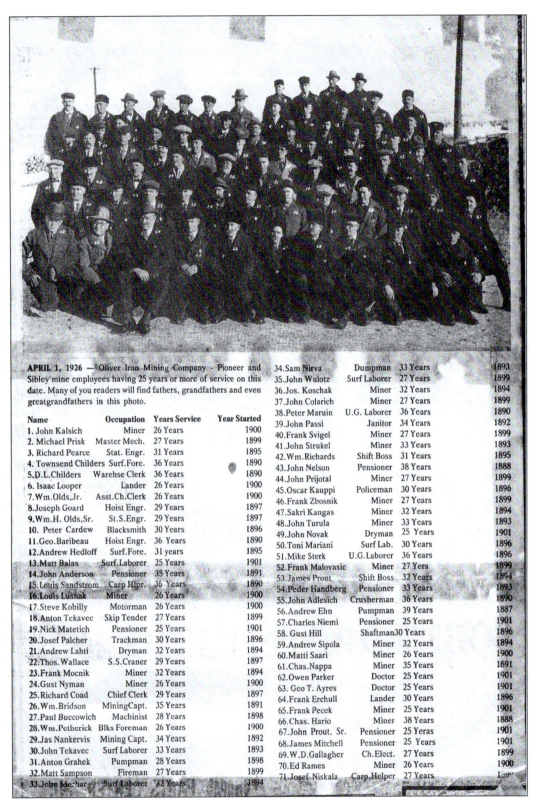

APRIL 1, 1926 — Oliver Iron Mining Company - Pioneer and Sibley mine employees having 25 years or more of service on this date. Many of you readers will find fathers, grandfathers and even greatgrandfathers in this photo.

Name	Occupation	Years Service	Year Started
1. John Kalsich	Miner	26 Years	1900
2. Michael Prisk	Master Mech.	27 Years	1899
3. Richard Pearce	Stat. Engr.	31 Years	1895
4. Townsend Childers	Surf.Fore.	36 Years	1890
5. D.L.Childers	Warehse Clerk	36 Years	1890
6. Isaac Looper	Lander	26 Years	1900
7. Wm.Olds,Jr.	Asst.Ch.Clerk	26 Years	1900
8. Joseph Goard	Hoist Engr.	29 Years	1897
9. Wm.H. Olds,Sr.	St.S.Engr.	29 Years	1897
10. Peter Cardew	Blacksmith	30 Years	1896
11. Geo.Baribeau	Hoist Engr.	36 Years	1890
12. Andrew Hedloff	Surf.Fore.	31 years	1895
13. Matt Balas	Surf.Laborer	25 Years	1901
14. John Anderson	Pensioner	35 Years	1891
15. Louis Sandstrom	Carp Hlpr.	36 Years	1890
16. Louis Lushak	Miner	26 Years	1900
17. Steve Kobilly	Motorman	26 Years	1900
18. Anton Tekavec	Skip Tender	27 Years	1899
19. Nick Matetich	Pensioner	25 Years	1901
20. Josef Palcher	Trackman	30 Years	1896
21. Andrew Lahti	Dryman	32 Years	1894
22. Thos.Wallace	S.S.Craner	29 Years	1897
23. Frank Mocnik	Miner	32 Years	1894
24. Gust Nyman	Miner	26 Years	1900
25. Richard Coad	Chief Clerk	29 Years	1897
26. Wm.Bridson	MiningCapt.	35 Years	1891
27. Paul Buccowich	Machinist	28 Years	1898
28. Wm.Petherick	Blks Foreman	26 Years	1900
29. Jas Nankervis	Mining Capt.	34 Years	1892
30. John Tekavec	Surf Laborer	33 Years	1893
31. Anton Grahek	Pumpman	28 Years	1898
32. Matt Sampson	Fireman	27 Years	1899
33. John Merhar	Surf Laborer	32 Years	1894
34. Sam Nirva	Dumpman	33 Years	1893
35. John Wulotz	Surf Laborer	27 Years	1899
36. Jos. Koschak	Miner	32 Years	1894
37. John Colarich	Miner	27 Years	1899
38. Peter Maruin	U.G. Laborer	36 Years	1890
39. John Passi	Janitor	34 Years	1892
40. Frank Svigel	Miner	27 Years	1899
41. John Strukel	Miner	33 Years	1893
42. Wm.Richards	Shift Boss	31 Years	1895
43. John Nelson	Pensioner	38 Years	1888
44. John Prijotal	Miner	27 Years	1899
45. Oscar Kauppi	Policeman	30 Years	1896
46. Frank Zbosnik	Miner	27 Years	1899
47. Sakri Kangas	Miner	32 Years	1894
48. John Turula	Miner	33 Years	1893
49. John Novak	Dryman	25 Years	1901
50. Toni Mariani	Surf Lab.	30 Years	1896
51. Mike Sterk	U.G. Laborer	36 Years	1896
52. Frank Malovasic	Miner	27 Yers	1899
53. James Prout	Shift Boss	32 Years	1894
54. Peder Handberg	Pensioner	33 Years	1893
55. John Adlesich	Crusherman	36 Years	1890
56. Andrew Ehn	Pumpman	39 Years	1887
57. Charles Niemi	Pensioner	25 Years	1901
58. Gust Hill	Shaftman	30 Years	1896
59. Andrew Sipola	Miner	32 Years	1894
60. Matti Saari	Miner	26 Years	1900
61. Chas.Nappa	Miner	35 Years	1891
62. Owen Parker	Doctor	25 Years	1901
63. Geo T. Ayres	Doctor	25 Years	1901
64. Frank Erchull	Lander	30 Years	1896
65. Frank Pecek	Miner	25 Years	1901
66. Chas. Hario	Miner	38 Years	1888
67. John Prout. Sr.	Pensioner	25 Yeras	1901
68. James Mitchell	Pensioner	25 Years	1901
69. W.D.Gallagher	Ch.Elect.	27 Years	1899
70. Ed Rames	Miner	26 Years	1900
71. Josef Niskala	Carp.Helper	27 Years	1899

Here are 71 employees of the Pioneer and Sibley mines, all of whom had at that time 25 or more years of service. Andrew Ehn is listed as a pump man with 39 years of service as of April 1, 1926. Presumably he came to Ely with service in another mine. At this point, mining in Ely had about forty more years before the end came on April 1, l967.

John Zobitz, Mike Klobuchar, Fred Pucel, and Joe Whiting in the underground "lunch room" of the Zenith Mine.

This miner who is believed to be a Mr. Skradski is preparing the dynamite that will be placed into holes that have been drilled into the ore body in the drift. Note the battery pack on his back which lights the lamp on his hard hat and the fact that his boots are wet. The miners often worked in dark and wet conditions.

Miners placing charges into holes bored into the ore deposit. The blast broke up the ore into chunks that could be loaded into the small ore cars called "skiffs" which were then brought to the surface of the mine and loaded onto the stockpiles. From there the ore was transferred into railroad cars and delivered to one of the loading docks in Two Harbors on Lake Superior. From there the ore was carried by large ore boats called "lakers" to the steel mills in the East. Note the "cribbing" —the timbers used to support the roofs of the mining tunnels.

Grand Rapids Herald-Review

Miners lined up "on surface" (above ground)—the boy and dog in the picture may indicate that he has come to bring his father's lunch. Note the wooden trestle overhead.

It was very, very seldom that anyone not directly connected with the mine was allowed underground. Safety and liability were big factors. This appears to be one of those rare occasions when women were permitted to be on the property (and presumably they had gone underground on a supervised tour). It would also be safe to assume they were either office employees of the mine or wives of staff personnel.

Men to the right are coming off the lift (called the "cage") and those on the left getting ready to descend to their working area underground (called the "drift). This is taken at the Sibley Mine which was operated by the Oliver Iron Mining Company in conjunction with the Pioneer Mine. The Sibley closed in the mid-1950s and the Pioneer in 1967.

It is unclear whether these men are just coming up or are about to descend. Either way, a ride on the "cage" was a noisy and often jerky ride.

At times labor unrest occurred in Ely. The signs of the picketing miners pretty much say it all. The picture is from the 1959 strike against United States Steel. The industry-wide strike was largely about wages.

One of the mine shafts is in the background. It is difficult to know whether the man standing outside the truck is being questioned or whether he is welcoming another who might be joining the picket line.

Prayer Candles

One of Mother's good friends, Joe Mismash, was trapped underground in a cave at the Pioneer Mine, and no one knew if he was dead or alive. The next thing I knew we were pulling on our coats and heading up to Saint Anthony's Church. When we got into the church it was already getting dark, and I could hear women's voices chanting in unison. It took a moment before my eyes adjusted to the dim light in the church but then I could see a group of women wearing black kerchiefs on their heads. They were all holding rosary beads in their hands, and they were chanting Hail Marys over and over again.

"What are they doing here?" I asked.

"They're praying, Michael. They always do when there is someone trapped underground. Most of those women have lost men to the mines, and they remember how terrible it was to have one of your men trapped underground. They will sit here and pray as long as the rescue miners are digging, and they will for as long as it takes."

Then we walked up the side aisle of the church to where the prayer candles were. Some of them were burning away in their red candleholders, and I thought they looked beautiful even if they didn't work. But then my mother did something I couldn't believe. She took a dollar bill out of her purse, pushed it into the collection box, and lit one of the big candles.

"I thought you told me that this was a silly superstition," I said as I looked at her by candlelight.

"Don't be stupid, Michael. My friend Joe is Catholic and if this candle does any good at all for him, then it is a dollar well spent. And furthermore we're going to come here every day and light a candle until we know that Joe's all right."

Mike Hillman
from *Stories of Old Ely &*
The Lake Country

Miners were given the opportunity to rent a "company house" from the mining company. Many of these homes were built in mining locations but there were other areas in town where there were clusters of company owned homes. One of these was the 900 block of East Sheridan St. and East Camp St. As mining operations expanded over the years, many of these homes were sold to the miners and moved onto vacant lots in residential areas of Ely. The superintendents and captains most often lived in much larger houses located on corner lots. The company houses were usu-ally two stories with three bedrooms and a bathroom. The earliest homes, such as those on Finn Hill or in Chandler Location did not originally have "indoor facilities." The yards were spacious enough for quite large vegetable gardens and even a small garage. The mining companies had a maintenance staff that looked after the mine buildings themselves but also did such things as painting the company houses.

The curtains, table, and wearing apparel all speak to the fact that this would be the living room of a miner's home probably in the first or second decade of the 1900s.

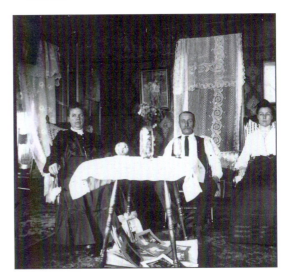

Families were often large and money was scarce. Slovenian families in particular had large vegetable gardens as is evidenced by this one which covers almost the entire yard of the Matesha family. Shown are son George, who became an accomplished classical pianist; Katherine, who was a secretary; and Victoria, who operated a fashionable ladies' apparel shop called "Vicky's," and father George. Lettuce, tomatoes, potatoes, cucumbers, squash, bush bean, pole beans, peppers, cabbage, carrots, peas, radishes, horseradish, dill, and pumpkins were among the things grown and canned or otherwise processed.

In order to keep the miners' homes near their workplaces, the mining companies built "locations." There were at least ten of them: Calumet, Sibley, Zenith, Pioneer, Chandler, "26," Spaulding, Finn Hill, Savoy, and the 900 block between Sheridan and Camp Streets. In most cases the mining company built the houses on their own property and rented them to the miners with families.

Most were three bedrooms. The earlier ones had no basements, central heat, or hot water. Nearly all of these houses were eventually sold to the tenants when the land beneath the buildings was to be mined. These houses were then moved onto empty lots in Ely proper. There were three or four basic house designs, the same ones used in other mining towns such as Aurora, Virginia, and Hibbing. In later years conditions and pay improved. Many miners were able to both buy a Buick and to send sons and daughters to college.

The company houses included two large triplexes and several duplexes, as well as the individual family homes. The triplexes from Calumet and Sibley were moved before WW II to the corner of James St. and Second Ave., as this picture shows. Years after when the houses had been moved, the abandoned mine property was sold to the City of Ely. In cases where there had been no mine tunnels dug, the location lots were sold and some new homes appeared.

This is the family of James Trezona, a family that came from Cornwall. On the right is Charles Trezona, who became Captain Trezona, the much feared and yet respected general superintendent of the Oliver Iron Mining Co. mines in Ely. It is for him that Ely's Trezona recreational trail is named.

The Oliver Iron Mining Co., which operated the Pioneer and Sibley mines, owned large acreages of timberland around Ely. Amongst those holdings were lands on Burntside Lake including Oliver Island. In 1914 a large log lodge was constructed for the use of company officials and special visitors. The local Girl Scout groups were also given permission to use it for their summer camps. It still stands but is now in private hands.

Sheave Wheels

The sheave wheels have stopped turning, on the head frame of the mine
No longer does the whistle blow to signal quitting time.
The dry house now is empty of clothes hung way up high
No laughing, joking miners playing in the dry.
The water seeping in the drift is filling up the sump,
But no longer can you hear the rhythm of the pump.
The ore chutes are all rotten, the rails thin lines of rust,
There's just a ghostly silence, spider webs and dust.
The sheave wheels have been turning on the headframe of the mine,
As long as I remember and before my time.
I often hurried to the mine when I was but a lad
And watched the sheave wheels turning while bringing lunch to dad.
Now twenty years I've labored, some miners twenty more,
And the sheave wheels kept on turning bringing up the ore.
There are empty houses on the street where I once did play,
The fellows that I worked with have packed and gone away.
Now this is my story of a changing time,
The sheave wheels have stopped turning on the head frame of the mine.

Leonard Koponen
Local 1922
Ironwood. Mich., 1965

When the last underground mine, the Pioneer, closed in 1967, the underground iron mining era came to an end. Only one mine shaft was left as a "monument" to what had happened there. According to one of the last mining engineers, water was pumped out at the rate of two thousand gallons per hour while the mine was operating. When they were turned off groundwater infiltrated the drifts (tunnels) and water quickly began to fill the tunnels. Eventually a number of them collapsed. Over time more sinking continued, creating the new "man made" lake now called Miner's Lake. The City of Ely obtained the mine property and has sold some of it to private individuals for homes and to businesses that located in the new business park. The five Ely mines, the Chandler, Pioneer, Savoy, Sibley, and Zenith were all connected underground. Water from the other mines drained into the Pioneer and miners wore rubber suits and boots.

Some of Ely's Retired Miners

◈ ◈ ◈

Johnny Barich

Fred Cherne

Dan Hestetune

Peter Jiacik

Jim Klobuchar

Stanley Kunstel

Adolph Levar

John Lindroos

Don Mikolich

Ray Nickolson

Barlo Portinen

Nick Przybylski

John Seliga

Joe Struna

John Vesel

He Was a Miner, A Dreamer, and My Father

In the mining towns' cauldron of nationalities and immigrant ambitions, the unalterable chemistry was this: that the children and grandchildren should have opportunity to grow and achieve in places more refined and more generous than the plain frame cloisters of the mining company locations where they lived.

Even in his last months, when he was weakened and tired, he produced something almost every day. And this morning in his house there are a half-dozen immaculately tilled little boxes of marigolds and snapdragons sprouting on the kitchen counter where he left them a few days ago.

The Cool Red Tunnels are Quiet

The idea of a college education for the children was an obsession with many of them and the reason they resisted when the son would plan to go underground to help raise money for it.

"Once you go down there," they would say, "'you will never get out."

Jim Klobuchar
from *Eight Miles Without a Pothole*

THE WORLD OF COMMERCE

◆ ◆ ◆

Probably the business in Ely that lasted the longest was the James Drug Store which was established in 1888 by Abijah James and Dr. Charles Shipman. When the Shipman hospital was built in 1895, Mr. James became the sole owner. The pharmacy business was purchased by the Pamida Corp. about 2000 and incorporated into its pharmacy. In the same picture is Agnew's Variety Store (the "dime store"). It was one of the most popular places in town for the young. Almost everything imaginable was sold here: goldfish, painted turtles, parakeets, yard goods, toys, confectionaries, household goods, some clothing, and most anything else that could be put into a bag. No meats, vegetables, or fruit, though!

Exterior of James Drug Store c. 1902. Dr. Charles Shipman first owned this building and operated an infirmary on the second floor. He and Abijah James established the pharmacy together on the street level, with Mr. James later becoming the sole owner. The space to the right has seen a number of businesses such as Agnew's Variety Store, Tauzell's Dept. Store, and finally it became part of the expanded James Drug.

The building now occupied by the Ely Ace Hardware was first built as a general mercantile by Otto Korb. Later, as this picture shows, the Berglund Brothers operated a similar business. Ace Hardware is now owned by the Merhar family.

Paul Martin was a Finnish immigrant who like a number of his compatriots who had a yen for business and established a long running jewelry store and watch and clock repair business on Chapman Street on a site now occupied by the State Farm Insurance agency. Besides selling and repairing timepieces of all kinds, the store sold diamond and gold jewelry, sterling silver serving pieces and flatware, and high quality dinnerware. In

later years his son-in-law ran the business, closing it about the time the Pioneer mine closed—a time when a number of family owned businesses lost too much of their clientele to stay in business.

In 1906 Jacob Lampi purchased the Ely Bottling Works from Otto Manninen. Prior to this Mr. Lampi had worked and then been injured in the mine so he left that job and purchased a saloon on Central Avenue. Although he retained ownership of that building, he let the building to Emil Forsman who continued the saloon business. Mr. Lampi lived in the large white clapboard house and bottled and sold soft drinks next door on Harvey St. He also ran a large logging operation. A Finnish immigrant, his soda pop was sold to businesses all over town. His secret recipe for crème soda was an all-time favorite in town. He passed that to his son Charlie, but Charlie took the recipe with him to his grave.

Gust A. Maki's Finnish immigrant father died of a ruptured appendix when Gust was twelve. At the age of fourteen, Gust went to work in the blacksmith shop at the Chandler mine. Local businessmen, Paddy Vail, recruited him as a clerk in his men's wear store. Twenty-five years later that business was sold and Gust began his own men's clothing store, Maki Clothing, which was in the family for forty years. Shown in this picture are Gust Maki and his nephew, Hugo "Clayboots" Kleemola.

Mike Weinzierl (on the left) served four terms as mayor, owned the first car dealership, and also a jewelry store. Picture is from about 1920 or a bit earlier. A. J. Thomas is pictured on the right.

Ely Hardware was established by John Harri, who later became one of Ely's early mayors. It occupied the building now known as Dee's Bar and Lounge, but the business had been sold to Louis Champa and Charles Merhar and was subsequently moved to the Berglund Bros. building on Chapman St. John and Andrew Harri were Finnish and Mr. Champa and Mr. Merhar were Slovenians, but they took along one of Harri's Finnish clerks, Pete Harri to accommodate the different ethnic clientele.

John Porthan, Andrew Watilo, and Eric Lund formed the Ely Finnish Stock Co. in 1900 as a corporation. A much larger building was constructed in 1914 (and is now the home of Steger Mukluks). This was a general mercantile dealing in fresh meats, groceries, dry goods, clothing, and some hardware. Its clientele were mostly Finns. Finnish speaking men went around the town each day to take orders for housewives and deliveries were made the same day. The store operated for nearly sixty years.

"Lawyer Thomas" (A. J. Thomas) was one of the town's early leading citizens, private practice attorney, city attorney, and a man active in any number of civic endeavors. This picture shows him in his office in June of 1925. Note the ornate wood-burning stove which appears to still being used.

August Haapala (aka "Hoppy") had a shoe repair shop on West Chapman St., but his talents did not end with that. He sewed pack sacks, tents, and sleeping bags. He fixed purses and repaired anything made of leather but absolutely no synthetics or foreign made goods of any kind. His granddaughter Sue Saari operated a weaving and yarn shop, Sisu Designs, there.

Although unidentified (as unfortunately so many pictures are), my best guess is that the man on the left is an early Ely businessman and the other perhaps a town official.

Otto Hokkanen, a Finnish immigrant, established the Cyko Art Studio and Camera Shop on Chapman St. He was one of a number of local photographers who did studio portrait work. For many decades during the 1900s nearly every high school senior had graduation pictures done in a local photo studio. Mr. Hokkanen was very knowledgeable about cameras and film and sold the whole line of Kodak and Agfa products. He was affectionately known as "Hokkie Otto."

One of Ely's iconic business establishments is the Ely Steam Bath on South First Avenue East. Built by Emil Ahola, a Finnish immigrant, in 1915, it has changed hands only once (other than family members). The concrete blocks used in its construction were made one at a time by Mr. Ahola. Although somewhat different than a traditional Finnish sauna, it has provided much the same experience for miners, families, and tourists. There is a men's room (the "Bull

Pen"), a ladies room (the "Hen House"), and several private room saunas. It has become quite popular as a place to clean up and relax for canoeists coming in from a trip into the boundary waters.

The Ely Theater opened in 1936 with a house that held 900 seats. It was built by the Baehr family who had movie theaters in other locales. Movies changed twice a week and on Saturday there was a special double feature for the younger crowd. It has been closed since the 1960s.

The building on the NW corner of Chapman and First Avenue East has had a long and varied history. It is known that a John Jackman had a confectionary and that he sold the building itself to the Knights and Ladies of Kaleva, a Finnish fraternal and cultural society. The main floor was later home to a number of businesses, among them a hardware store, a millinery shop, a dress shop, women's clothing store, and most lately an antiques consignment store. Although the Knights of Kaleva has sold the building and disbanded, the Ladies of Kaleva are still active in 2014.

Originally the Central Garage was owned by a Mr. Kurvinen, a Finn. It was later purchased by John Koshak, Jr., a Slovenian. He sold Buicks and GMC trucks, serviced them, and sold gasoline for decades, into his later 80s. Many miners bought Buicks and Pontiacs here because John convinced them they would hold up better than anything else. Many young people bought second hand cars here for their first vehicles. For many years John Koshak had the only wrecker service in town and was an AAA provider. He pulled innumerable cars out of the snow and from ditches over the years.

Pete's Garage was built by Jacob Pete in the 1920s, on a site that once was occupied by Cormack's store and the Chandler House hotel. Mr. Pete was another of the early Finnish entrepreneurs who had a number of business interests. Besides this building, in which a Dodge and Plymouth agency was located, there also were other offices including those for an attorney. Jacob Pete also operated a logging company, a resort, and Pete's Cabin Boats on Basswood Lake. He also served as a county commissioner for many years.

Mike Motors, begun by Mike Weinzierl, pumped gas, serviced cars and trucks, and was the Studebaker dealer in town. The agency now sells General Motors and Jeep vehicles.

Cities Service is now a Cenex gas station and convenience store. It was originally opened by a Swede/Finn immigrant, Amelius Stenlund. It was one of at least a dozen "filling stations" that were in evidence in Ely throughout the better part of the twentieth century.

The Miller Store building on Chapman St. no longer exists but it opened as the Dobie Bros. and Miller Mercantile in 1888. It carried first class merchandise such as groceries, ladies and men's apparel, and dry goods and catered to the salaried mining personnel, school and city officials, etc. In other words, the working class, although not discouraged as customers, seldom shopped there. R.S Miller shortly became the sole proprietor and later his brother, Thomas E. Miller, took over the business. T. E. Miller also was the federal Indian Agent for this area.

Stanley and Tony Klun operated a grocery store and meat market that was begun by their immigrant parents. It originally served a largely Slovenian clientele. It is now co-owned by Tony's granddaughter, Kelly Klun and Gordon and Gail Sheddy and is operated as a restaurant called A Taste of Ely.

One of many family owned grocery stores that operated through the 1950s in Ely, Skala's specialized in fresh meats. Eventually the store building was incorporated into an expanded Zupancich Bros. store (before it moved to its present location across the street). Many of these stores had their own "ethnic" clientele—this one being Slovenian.

John Zupancich, Sr., who was born in Slovenia, established a grocery store on the SE corner of E. Third Avenue and Sheridan St. The store expanded to the east two different times and eventually built a large supermarket across the street. Brothers John, Jr., Leonard, Albert, and Ed took over the operation and eventually built Zup's stores in Cook, Tower, Silver Bay, and Babbitt. The fourth generations are now in charge.

The meat counter at the former site of Zup's. The store became famous for their sausages, particularly hot bologna.

The Ely Bowling Center was owned and operated for many years by Lee and John "Pecksy" Perushek. It was gathering place for meeting friends, socializing, and provided a form of recreation that was especially popular during the long winter months for men, women, and youth.

One of many smaller eating establishments that were prevalent in mid twentieth century Ely. Quite a few of them catered to single men (loggers and miners) and to the single school teachers whose homes were rented rooms in town.

Ed Hill's pool hall was an early Ely fixture on E. Chapman St., next to what was the Elco Theater, and now the site of the Masonic building. The miners and loggers worked hard, played hard, and drank hard. Theirs was a hard and often dangerous life.

A gathering place of a slightly different nature just down a block from the Bowling Center was Mavetz' Bar. It had once been known as the First and Last Chance Saloon as it was just opposite the railroad station. A popular patron was a little Italian named Jimmy Viglio. It has been said that at one time there were more than thirty bars, saloons, or taverns in Ely. A few also sold food such as steak dinners. These "watering holes" were places where primarily men gathered to unwind and socialize after long hard shifts in the mine. It can not be overlooked that the rate of alcoholism in Ely was rather high during the mining era.

For many years the Greyhound bus line extended to Ely and for a number of those years there were two busses in and out each day. One long-time and well-liked driver was Albert Mutka, shown here second from the left. The bus was a life line to the outside world in the days before people had their own cars.

The northwest corner of Second Avenue and Sheridan Street was once home to Kovall's grocery store. Later it became a Piggly Wiggly market and Rik's Inn, an eatery, bakery, cafeteria, and Greyhound bus depot. After the Forest Hotel burned in December of 1967, which also housed Vertin's Café, Matt Vertin Jr. renovated the Rikhus building into a café, dining room, and pub. It was a popular eatery (bus service had long since disappeared from Ely) for a number of years, changing hands several times. It closed in 2009 but at this writing has been purchased by a new developer.

Mary Z. Palcher was in later years one of the prominent business women in Ely. Her husband started a clothing store on the corner of Central Avenue and Sheridan St. in the 1940s. She had her shoe store in the back of the building off the avenue side. After Joseph Palcher died, Mary and her two sisters-in-law ran both businesses. In the late 1950s Mary re-invented her business as Palcher's Town and Country Shop and moved onto Chapman St. It carried high quality merchandise for women. She was known as "Mary Z. Palcher" as there were two other Mary Palchers in town.

Peter Schaefer had a long run with newspapers beginning in Tower in 1888 and then two years later in Ely. In 1895 he established the Ely Miner. It was the major player in Ely news until ceasing publication in 1986. The local newspapers of the day included much more than city council news, police reports, and obituaries. Weddings were big news with every possible detail incorporated into an article with a large picture of either the couple or just the bride. Those who "motored" out of town on business or visitors who came to town were events reported in the paper column called "Round and About Town." A whole page by the "society" editor mentioned all sorts of meetings and even local bridge club gatherings (who came, what was served, and who received "honors" in the game). Mr. Schaefer is shown in the far right of this picture. Following his untimely death, his nephew, Fred Childers, took over the paper. He in turn was succeeded upon his death by his wife, Columbia Paris Childers until 1986.

Begun as a drive in root beer stand by Eddie and Annamae Pucel in the 1950s, the A and W expanded into a sit-in restaurant. It was a fixture especially for local teenagers for nearly thirty years. It eventually became a Subway restaurant.

Wilderness Outfitters was the in-town base for Basswood Lodge. Resorts on the wilderness lakes sprung up largely after WW II. Within twenty years they began to be things of the past as new legislation to preserve and protect (and to some extent restore) the wilderness area was passed. These remote resorts and fishing camps were accessible by canoe, motor boats, motor launches, amphibious "ducks," and float planes. The new legislation prohibited float planes and nearly all motorized craft. This caused dissension in the community that has never been completely resolved. One of the many reasons men returned to Ely and the mines after WW II was the access to fishing and camping in the wilderness area close to Ely.

WELY was the local radio station operated by Charles Persons. It is now owned by the Bois Forte Band of Chippewa.

The Kainz brothers, Leo, Ray, and Norman, began one of the "latter day" sawmills a few miles east of town on Highway 88. It operated from 1962 and into the 1980s

The "Old Central School" class of 1906. The children in this photo represent many ethnic backgrounds: Finnish, Swedish, Slovenian, English, and probably some German and Polish. The young girl who is first on the left in the third row is Helia Koski. She went on to become a much admired long-term teacher in the Lincoln Elementary School.

Schools – The Pride of Ely

There were schools in the Ely area going back as far as 1888, the first known one being a "homesteader" school on the North Arm of Burntside Lake. The first grammar school in Ely itself was located on the site of the present Community Center building. It was built in 1889 but by 1892 a second story was added to accommodate the growing number of students. It was then named the Central School. The first high school was Pioneer School, also a frame building built in 1899. The buildings that followed, the Lincoln School, the Old High, the Washington School, and the Memorial High School, were all substantial brick buildings with accommodations that would have been the envy of any number of other Minnesota schools.

The Memorial High School building was completed in 1924 at a cost of $1,000,000. It contained, beside classrooms and offices, a swimming pool, two gymnasiums, science laboratories and a greenhouse, fully equipped home economics facilities, a library with a separate reference library room, and spaces for a school doctor, nurse, and dentist. In an adjacent building were accommodations for a band and orchestra and industrial arts classrooms and shops. Marble, oak, brass, and gold leaf were incorporated into the design. A stage and auditorium seating 900 was located in the adjoining Washington building and the various buildings on the campus were connected with underground tunnels. The grounds were beautifully landscaped with raised gardens, trees, well-groomed shrubbery, and paved curved walkways evoking a park-like landscape. A school newspaper and annual yearbook were established in the early 1920s. In 1922 Ely established the second junior college in Minnesota. Educational credits earned here were accepted without question by the University of Minnesota when students transferred to a four-year degree program.

It should be pointed out that the upper echelon of the mining staff had a vision for their children that they would have all the advantages of schools in larger and more settled parts of the country. Thus the mining companies, in their heyday, could be counted on to financially support the schools. The bar for qualified teachers was set high. Textbooks and school supplies were provided at no cost. Along with this however was a philosophy that the school children from homes of immigrants were to be "homogenized" in the education process. Thus children who spoke a foreign language such as Finnish, Slovenian, Italian, or one of the Scandinavian languages were even punished when they did not speak English.

Patriotism was doled out in heavy dosages. Students were given textbook covers featuring a Liberty bell and the Pledge of Allegiance. There was a picture of either George Washington or Abraham Lincoln or both in every classroom as well as an American flag. The Pledge was recited faithfully every morning. During the War Years and even after defense stamps (used to purchase war bonds) were sold every Tuesday morning.

Early scene from the Central School. These young children with their folded hands appear both so innocent and well behaved.

Central School was built in 1892 and expanded with a second story the next year.

More young children at their desks at the Central School. Note how many of the girls are wearing white dresses. With the closing of the Central School these desks were moved to the new Washington Elementary and were still in use in the early 1950s.

Eight teachers are posed in front of the first school building in Ely, the Central School. The school served Ely students from 1889 – 1921. Shortly after it was used as a public library and then razed in the mid-1930s to make way for the new Community Center building.

The Bureau of Indian Affairs established an Indian boarding school at Lake Vermilion in the early part of the twentieth century (pictured in 1906). Agents, sometimes even Indian ones, did their best to convince parents their children were better off being taken to board and be educated there. Conditions were often harsh for these young children. They were punished for speaking to one another in their native tongue.

The Pioneer School was the first high school in Ely.

Some of the older students at Pioneer School. The Pioneer Apartments are located now on that site. There appear to be three teachers in the back, one of whom is a man.

In the same year as the Lincoln School was built—1905—a new high school building was constructed. It functioned as a high school for less than twenty years until the newer and much lager Memorial High School opened in 1924. The young immigrant miners were now producing families, many of them rather large, and the mines were in full production. The 1905 building became known as "Old High" which was used for junior high students. In 1922 Ely Junior College took over the top two floors, still sharing the lower levels with some of the junior high students.

To accommodate the growing school population, the very substantial Lincoln School opened in 1905. It served as an elementary school through 1976. The site is now occupied by a new assisted living facility that retained the Lincoln name.

The Old High was constructed in 1905 and a machine shop area was located on the basement level. This shows a class of boys in 1918.

Sixteen high school graduates were given their diplomas in 1915 with an elaborate backdrop at the Washington Elementary School Auditorium. Apparently it was acceptable for both the boys and girls to wear hats and caps.

Eighth grade was the end of a formal education for many students at that time and graduation ceremonies were held to mark the occasion. Note the much larger number of student compared to the 1915 high school graduating class. One of them was John Kapsch, who went further with his education and became a long term municipal judge.

This class graduated during the height of the Great Depression in 1937. It is obvious some of the graduates did not have the means to buy suits as later graduates did, but their apparel would certainly be perfectly acceptable today. The author's mother appears in the middle of the picture. She raised six sons who all graduated from this same school and she herself went on to become a teacher after becoming a young widow.

Sigurd Olson taught biological sciences at the high school and junior college before becoming the Dean of the college and later a well known author. Shown here is the Ely Junior College Class of 1938. Ely Junior College was for many years a part of the local school district but in 1964 it came under the jurisdiction of the State of Minnesota.

This graduating class from 1943 with their graduation gowns indicates how things have recovered from the Depression. Sigurd Olson is the Dean and academic head of the Junior College. Marion Rautio Cherne became a teacher and Ruth Yadlosky Zaverl became an R.N. both of them women in this class with immigrant backgrounds.

Idelia Loso was a much admired Dean of the Junior College. She was the first woman in the state to serve as the administrative head of a community college. She had a very hands-on approach in managing the curriculums of individual students, with an eye to see that the academic credits of each student would transfer readily to other institutions of higher learning. Students called her "Mother Loso" but not to her face.

A surprising number of Ely High School graduates went on into the "greater world" and gained recognition in their fields. Among them was Joy Wilmunen who became the publicity director and an editor for the Harvard Press. As a child she suffered from a seventy percent hearing loss but from her mother, a teacher, she learned to lip read. Before there were programs for handicapped students, teachers had to fill in the gaps somehow. Joy graduated as valedictorian of her class and graduated from Hamline University and Smith College with high honors before becoming associated with Harvard. Her teachers were no doubt proud of her success, but Ely can be proud of the schools that played a role in this story.

In 1959, with the mining still the backbone of the economy, the JFK building opened. It housed a new elementary school and an expanded Ely Junior College. The junior college now had its own space for many new activities, including this fencing team coached by James Hiner.

The junior college had its own athletes such as Joe Fink.

"Pete" Moroni also coached the Junior College team. Many students at the "JC" came from area schools such as Tower, Soudan, Babbitt, and Embarrass, but very few came from out of state unlike the student population in the 2000s.

Athletics were a part of the educational scene very early. Shown here is a basketball team from 1919. None of the players or their coach is identified.

Note the uniforms for this baseball team presumably from the late 'teens or very early 1920s. The bat boy was John Somrock who later became known as "Judge Shammy," one of Ely's municipal judges.

Ely High School baseball team from the 1920s. The small houses in the background were moved and the grounds beautifully landscaped much like a park. Most of this was given up in the 1950s for the construction of the JFK Elementary School and addition to the junior college. The baby boomers were now of school age, the mines were at near full employment, and the nearby taconite mines were opening.

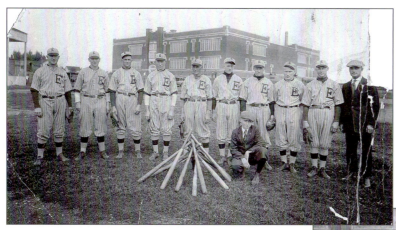

Coach Peter Moroni's winning basketball team shown with their district high school championship trophy.

A very early Ely High School football team. Their names are evidence of Finnish, English, Slovenian, German, and Cornish background.

As soon as the new Memorial High School opened in 1924, complete with a swimming pool, swimming appeared as part of the curriculum and as a competitive sport. There were both boys' and girls' swimming teams. Shown in this picture from 1925-1926 with Coach Max Herseth are twelve young men. Nine have a Finnish background and three are Slovenian. The proportion of the Finns is undoubtedly due to the abundance of lakes back in the land of their forefathers.

SWIMMING TEAM 1925-26
Left to right:
J. Pucel, E. Jokinen, W. Nappa, E. Tantari,
J. Bezek, A. Winnikainen, L. Pogorelc,
U. Hokkanen, E. Laitala, H. Pappanen, Uno Saari,
W. Thompson, Coach Max Herseth

(Property of Uno Saari)

Leonard Klun is shown on the right. He won the State Championship in Diving in 1935 and became a long-time and much admired swimming teacher and coach in Ely (and his heritage was Slovenian). His 1949 team won the state championship.

Long time coach Edward Buckley with one of his basketball teams. Ed Buckley had a long coaching career and his teams took a number of district championships and went on to the state level.

These girls were basketball champions in 1926. It likely was a district championship.

Girls competed in basketball from some of the earliest days of a high school in Ely. Irene Thomas was the daughter of "Lawyer" Thomas, a prominent pioneer city father.

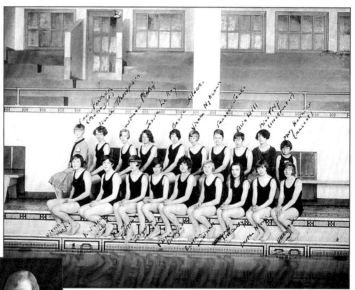

The 1927-1928 girls' swimming team also had a preponderance of Finns but proportionately less than the boys. Their coach is Miss Trip.

Eight girls and their coach who were the 1929-1930 (presumably district) champions in girls' basketball. Girls' teams continued on into the 1930s under the GAA (Girls' Athletic Association). Interscholastic competition resumed in 1973.

The 1960s were the glory days of ice hockey at EHS. The team won several district championships and in 1964, under Capt. David Merhar, won the region and went on to state competition. The picture shown is one with most of those team members when they were not yet in high school.

Ely had a ski jumping slide on the west side of town as early as 1921. It was later replaced by a much larger one at Hidden Valley.

Ely skiers head off to the ski jump at Hidden Valley.

The Lincoln School rink was a popular rink for many years. The rink in the background was the hockey rink.

"Teeny – Weeny Band" in 1937. The music program was big in numbers and first-rate in quality under Mr. De Nino. Students began lessons early on in grade school and this group was the feeder group for the band and orchestra in the high school.

The high school in Ely offered music education in the form of vocal choirs, individual instrumental lessons, band, and full orchestra including stringed instruments. The ensemble pictured here is from the 1920s. At the piano is Lillian Schaeffer Wenstrom, daughter of the local newspaper publisher. She was active in Ely musical circles well into her 80s. The drummer, Carl Johnson, whose parents had come from Sweden, moved to Ely in 1914 possibly because of the outstanding educational opportunities here.

Mr. Frank De Nino put together a high school band and an orchestra that had an extremely high reputation throughout northern Minnesota. He is shown here in an undated picture in the Washington Auditorium in the late 1930s or early 1940s.

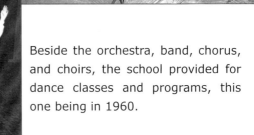

Beside the orchestra, band, chorus, and choirs, the school provided for dance classes and programs, this one being in 1960.

High school homecoming was a big event for both football and basketball. A homecoming queen and king were elected by the sophomores, juniors, and seniors.

A high school football team from 1952.

A young Jim Toms from the 1940s. James Toms went on to become a career Naval Officer.

The names of Vertin, Kauppi, and Polombi (Slovenian, Finnish, and Italian) indicate the ethnic diversity still prevalent in the 1950s.

Golf had a place in high school athletics but it waxed and waned over the years. Ely had some outstanding golfers beginning again in the 1960s.

The class proms were a big event beginning in the 1950s. The girls then all wore floor length gowns and while the boys all wore suits, none here appear to have worn tuxedos.

John Perko presenting Loyal Order of the Moose Scholarship Award. Almost all the local fraternal and ethnic organizations sponsored scholarships for local high school graduates as it often was one of their goals to see to the advancement of sons, daughters, and local students.

Local attorney Willard Domich is presenting the V.F.W. Science Award to Donald Diedrich.

This looks to be the end of the school year and the start of a new adventure as these young men wave from a car in front of the high school in the early 1950s. Young men really had several choices beyond high school: to attend the highly accredited local junior college, to work (for rather good wages) "down in the hole," or to join the military. There were not many other jobs available besides general labor or logging.

Ely's Churches

Church Corner, Sunday, 1955, watercolor by Russell Sawdey

Within the first ten years of mining in Ely, large numbers of immigrants flocked to town and within less than ten years three Lutheran churches, a Catholic, a Presbyterian, and a Methodist church were all organized. Shortly afterwards one of the Finnish Lutheran churches split into two. These churches were largely representative of the ethnic backgrounds of the population. Roughly forty percent of the population came from a Finnish (and mostly Lutheran) heritage, another forty percent were of a Slovenian (and Catholic) heritage, and perhaps twenty percent from other minorities. The first religious gatherings were in homes and Sunday Schools for children followed next. It would be fifty years later before two new denominations entered the scene.

The picture of this small wooden church shows a building on what is now Washington St. It was the "home" of four different Lutheran congregations. The Finnish Independent Lutheran Church began here but later moved to a new larger building on Camp St. In 1902 the Suomi Synod group split off and established their own church. The original small church building was later sold to the Apostolic or Laestadian Lutherans. After they disbanded the original group of people who formed the Gospel Tabernacle used the building in the late 1940s. It has since been dismantled.

This picture was taken on church corner where the Swedish Lutheran church (shown on left), the Catholic church (on right), the Methodist church (whose picket fence is in the foreground), and one Finnish Lutheran church (not shown but to the right of the Catholic church) once stood. The Methodist church (1895) is still standing. The Swedish church was razed in 1963 when the Swedes merged with other Finns. The Catholic church was razed when a new edifice was built across the street in 1958. The one Finnish Lutheran church built its new building further east on Camp St. in 1969. The location is Third Avenue East and Camp Street and the funeral procession is headed toward the Catholic church.

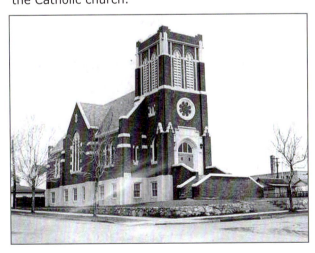

In 1902 a schism split the original Lutheran congregation and a group left to form the Suomi Synod Church. Meeting first in the Bethany Swedish Lutheran Church, they built a "basement church" (Our Savior's Lutheran) on the corner of Third Avenue East and Conan St. in 1925. The sanctuary and upper level were not completed until 1941. Bethany Lutheran merged with Our Savior's in 1963 and was henceforth called Grace Lutheran joining what had been separate Finnish and Swedish Lutheran churches. It became part of the ELCA.

First Lutheran Church began as the Finnish Independent Lutheran Church in 1890. The first church was a small frame building on Washington St. It moved to a new building on Camp St. in 1899. In 1968 the congregation built a new brick building in the 900 block of Camp St. It was known as the National Lutheran Church for some time but in the 1930s it affiliated with the Missouri Synod.

Bethany Lutheran church was formed in 1902 by a largely Swedish and a smaller Norwegian group of immigrants. It became affiliated with the (Swedish) Augustana Conference in 1906. In 1963 they merged with the Finns to form Grace Lutheran Church. The church had added an educational building by moving the former White Iron school into town and joining it with the church building. Both buildings were demolished shortly after the merger in 1963. The upper right picture shows the stee-

ple of the Bethany church and the above left is of the three neighboring churches (Bethany Lutheran, St. Anthony's Catholic, and First Lutheran – all since razed). The lower photo is of the Bethany Vacation Bible School from the 1930s.

The First Presbyterian Church was the first to organize a nondenominational Sunday School (upstairs of a local tavern it was said). It then formally organized as a church in 1888. The first building was built on the south side of Harvey St. in 1890, then at the far edge of town. In 1924 this frame building was moved off the site to James St. and a brick edifice, designed by Oliver Iron Mining Co. engineers, was erected. The charter members were largely of English and Scottish origin, but the nondenominational Sunday School later brought in others of other ethnic Protestant backgrounds.

An interior view of the Ely United Methodist Church.

The Methodists in Ely were largely of English (especially Cornish) extraction, many of them products of the tin mines in Cornwall. The church building was constructed in 1892-1893 and is still being used today. As such it is the only original church building in the city.

St. Anthony's Catholic Church was at first a mission church of St. Martin's Catholic Church in Tower. The first baptism here was in November of 1888. Under the leadership of missionary Fr. Joseph F. Buh, the first church building for the parish was constructed in 1890 on the site of the present rectory. It was a small frame structure that was used for only ten years. In 1900 Fr. Buh (later Msgr.) was given the full time assignment of the Ely church, where he was much beloved by his parishioners and served until 1922.

This young lady is in First Communion attire, complete with candle, prayer card, and flowers.

An unidentified young man also in First Communion attire. Note the knickers. Beside the candle he is holding a book and possibly a rosary.

Funeral for a young woman at the Catholic Church, likely showing her widowed husband behind and Fr. Buh with two young daughters to the right. Especially in the first decades of the 1900s, it was not uncommon for one of the parents to die rather young. There followed, with a second marriage of the surviving spouse, many blended families.

Pictured here is the interior of the 1900 church with a wedding in progress on April 19, 1947. The statues and other embellishments were due to the work of Fr. Buh. The building accommodated 500 persons and was used until 1958.

By 1897 the parish had grown rapidly and a full time priest was assigned for the Ely church. By 1900, when the parish had grown to 1900 members, a new church building was constructed under the direction of Fr. Andrew Smrekar. This new building was directly across the street of the first building.

Three women from St. Anthony's Catholic church preparing food presumably for a church dinner.

The Confraternity of Christian Doctrine school at St. Anthony's was the result of Fr. Frank Mihelcic's efforts. He is shown here with Sister Andrina Kvaternik on the left and Sister Maxine Erchul and Jane Veranth on the right. Standing are Frances Perushek and Sister Marcella Cartie. Fr. "Mike" pastored a church for nearly forty percent of the local population. He retired in 1968 and died in 1980.

Built in 1957-1958 the new church building is located just to the east of the original 1890 building. It was built under the direction of Fr. Frank Mihelcic during his fortieth year as the pastor. Brick on the outside, the sanctuary is faced with Italian Travertine marble. It accommodates 800 people.

Because the first city cemetery on the south edge of town proved to be on private land, the city needed to secure land for a new one on the east end of town. At the time this was about a half mile from the school campus, which was itself really the edge of town. The year was 1900. Shown are three new graves in the new cemetery. The large cross in the background was for the Catholic portion of the cemetery (Yes, there was an informal kind of segregation between Catholics and Protestants.). As was the custom in Europe, there were fences around many of the graves.

The Ely Baptist church was the last of the Ely churches to organize during the "mining era"—in 1953. A church building was constructed on the corner of Third Avenue East and Boundary St. and later a larger newer one was built on East Camp St.

The Gospel Tabernacle first held services at the small church building on Washington St. that had originally been the Finnish Lutheran church. In 1952 a new building was constructed on South Central Avenue near the golf course.

The Gospel Tabernacle and Ely Baptist Church did not organize until nearly fifty years had passed since the earlier churches had organized before or just after 1900. During later decades the population of the town gradually became more diverse. In the years following the end of the mining era in 1967 a number of other churches came on the scene. These later churches were not dominated by any single ethnic group as were the earlier ones.

Health Care in Ely

Abijah James established the first pharmacy in Ely in a building that still stands on Chapman St. and First Avenue East. (See photo on page 33). With the help and encouragement of Dr. Charles Shipman he opened an infirmary above the pharmacy. It served as the first hospital in the frontier mining town of Ely. Over the eighty years as a mining town Ely saw the construction of the Shipman Hospital and then the Ely-Bloomenson Community Hospital. Besides these there were also the Tanner Hospital and the Winton Hospital, all of these built to accommodate the needs of a growing community. In the early days mining accidents were frequent and often tragic and over the years the mining companies were more involved in supporting the medical community. Although routine treatments and surgeries were regularly done locally, more serious cases were referred to Virginia and Duluth.

The Shipman Hospital was built by Dr. Charles Shipman in 1895 having been designed by the doctor's father. It was located on Chapman St. across from the City Hall and it served as the city hospital until 1958. Drs. Shipman, Ayres, Parker, and Sutherland were the four "pioneer physicians" at the hospital. The staff attended to thousands of babies born there as well as many injured in mining and logging accidents. The hospital had an elevator which served all three floors of the hospital as well as the basement where the kitchen and lab were located.

Mary Pruukki (aka Pruki) was known widely as a midwife and assisted Dr. Shipman at his hospital She was left a widow at age forty with four children. They lived on a homestead at White Iron.

Maria Hario (also known as "Emmi") with her grandson Walter Leino, Sr. Mrs. Hario lived in the part of town known as "Finn Hill." She was widowed early in her marriage and became a well-known midwife. Her great grandson, Walter Leino, Jr., became a medical doctor and practiced in Ely for nearly forty years.

Dr. Antero Tanner's hospital on Camp St. was built in 1902. A private hospital, it was said to be the most modern and up-to-date in all of Northeast Minnesota. It was sold in 1907 to a Dr. Carpenter. He also had it for only a short time—until 1914. Eventually it closed and became a rooming house, an apartment house, student housing, and now stands empty.

Back in the 1930s when there were still serious epidemics of infectious diseases such as whooping cough, smallpox, and diphtheria the city constructed a small two story plus basement "detention hospital" whose purpose was to isolate or quarantine primarily children who were ill with one of these diseases. Equipped with a laboratory and a kitchen it was very much underused. After being essentially vacant for a number of years the building was leased to the US Department of the Interior for research pertaining to the Shagawa Lake Eutrophication Project. It was later razed to make space for the expansion of the Ely-Bloomenson Community Hospital Nursing Home—now Boundary Waters Care Facility.

The Ely-Winton Memorial Hospital was first built just after 1900 as an elementary school for the children of the employees of the Swallow Hopkins Lumber Co. It continued as a school until 1940. In 1949 Dr. O. E. Snyker remodeled the building into a hospital. It operated as a hospital until closing in 1967, the same year the last mine in Ely closed. It later became a convent retreat house and then student housing. It eventually burned down in 1980.

Dr. Harry Sutherland greets some of the more than 3000 babies he has delivered since coming to Ely in 1912. On the far left are Mrs. John Seliga and her children Jerome and Jean, representing two generations and three of the 3000 babies. A celebration and commemorative dinner were held in his honor in September of 1952.

Dr. Sutherland and Stephen Grahek, the 3000th baby. The first was Rose Lobe Mackie.

The new Ely-Bloomenson Community Hospital opened in 1958. $100,000 was donated to its construction by former Ely businessman Abe Bloomenson and $50,000 was given by Reserve Mining. A bond issue for $550,000 for construction was passed by the City of Ely.

Dr. Harry N. Sutherland sees his dream come true—a new modern hospital—as he cuts the ribbon at the entrance on February 22, 1958.

Clubs, Organizations, Lodges, & Fraternal Orders

The small town of Ely was peppered with organizations of many kinds. The country in general was more into the mode of ethnic, fraternal, and religious organizations beginning after WW I and continuing on into the 1970s and 1980s. The list is long—more than forty—and reflects how involved with organizations the townspeople were during this time: Veterans of Foreign Wars and Ladies Auxiliary, American Legion Post and Ladies Auxiliary, Jaycees and Mrs. Jaycees, Knights of Columbus, Sweet Adelines, Catholic Orders of Foresters and Women Foresters, Ely Catholic Women, Oddfellows and Rebekahs, Freemasons and Order of the Eastern Star, Job's Daughters, Chamber of Commerce, Rotarians, Kiwanians, American Fraternal Union, Ely Musicale, Ely Business and Professional Women, Music and Drama, Rod and Gun Club, Knights and Ladies of Kaleva, Vesi Temperance Society, American Association of University Women, Dillonaires/Drum and Bugle Corps, Boy Scouts and Girl Scouts, Slovenian Women's Union, Dawn Club, Assumption of the Blessed Virgin Lodge, Croatian Fraternal Women, Slovence Lodge, Immaculate Conception Lodge, N.A.B.A. Women's Lodge, S. N. P. J. , Loyal Order of the Moose, Scandinavian Fraternity, labor unions…and still others now part of the past.

A service club of long standing was the Kiwanis Club. It might appear that women were members at the time this picture was taken in the late 1940s or early 1950s but that did not happen until later. Organized in Ely in 1939, it supported youth organizations, civic projects, and provided annual scholarships for high school graduates.

Otto Brownell, proprietor of a flourishing meat market, also had a summer home on an island in Burntside Lake. He and some of his friends organized the "Ash Barrel Club"—an informal group of men whose main object was a rather impressive four-day outing on the island in the middle of the winter. The menu was amazing: beaver tail, venison, moose hump, turkey, and lobster, salmon, clams, and oysters shipped in wooden barrels from out East. It lasted from 1891 – 1905.

The Ladies of Kaleva, an organization for Finnish women, was organized in 1905. It is still active today in 2014 and is the oldest chapter in the U.S. and Canada. It, like other ethnic organizations, was intent on keeping the traditions of the land of their forefathers alive in this county, as well as fostering the education and advancement in society of its members. The Ladies and the Knights of Kaleva had their own meeting hall and a summer lodge on Burntside Lake.

"The Old Photograph Album" was a play put on by the local Eastern Star women (supplemented by a few Masons).

The Veterans of Foreign Wars acquired this building for their club after the Jugoslav National Home built a new building on Chapman St. Prior to that, the building had been a bar operated by the I.W.W. (International Workers of the World). The post at one time had 500 members. Beside the camaraderie

they enjoyed as veterns, the service organizations gave back much to the community in scholarships, youth activities, and fund-raising for worthy causes such as cancer research.

Women in town found a social outlet in various clubs and organizations such as the Music and Drama Club, the Ely Musicale, The Order of the Eastern Star, the Rebekahs, card clubs such as bridge and canasta, and church groups. Included in this picture are the wives of two of the mining superintendents and other prominent citizens. The lady with the "widest" smile was Helen ("Nell") Hanson, or Mrs. E.W. Hanson, as she would have been known all of her adult life. She was a real club woman, the organist in the Presbyterian church, and the wife of a mayor. Her sister, Ruth Nankervis, was the city librarian, and her father was the Rev. Blackhurst, who served both the Methodist and Presbyterian churches.

Some groups were organized by gender, some by ethnicity, and others by religious affiliation. The Slovenian Ladies Union met at St. Anthony's church. It formed at least partly to preserve the culture and traditions of Slovenia, the homeland of many early immigrant women.

This was as group of nearly all Slovenian Catholic women who for some unknown reason organized a drill team. The picture is from 1940.

The Slovenian Choir is shown here in about the late 1960s. Note the national costumes and the mine shaft in the background. This tells a lot about the town.

The American Legion (and the Veterans of Foreign Wars) organized with the vets returning from WW II. This was the era of "joining" and many organizations flourished in this small town. The Legion members marched as an impressive body in the Fourth of July and some special parades. They supported scholarships, youth activities, and the needs of veterans.

The women's contingent of the Legion was called the Auxiliary. They marched in the parades as a unit and were active in the schools for American Education Week. They, like the Legionaires, raised money for local scholarships, supported youth activities, faithfully sold poppies on Poppy Days, and supported disabled veterans wherever they could.

Past Presidents of the American Legion Auxiliary—from the many represented here, one can see this organization has continued for many decades.

Veterans got together to feed themselves and the public—some of these feeds were just for the veterans, but occasionally they were fundraisers. Proceeds went to help youth activities such as summer camps, scout troops, sports teams (particularly baseball), and scholarship awards to graduating high school seniors. Donations were made by the VFW, the Legion, and the women's auxiliaries for research for various serious diseases and to help the families of veterans in need.

The veterans sponsored Boy Scout troops such as this one—#174, which still exists in Ely in 2014. Patriotism was very much a part of veterans' organizations and they sought to see that it was instilled in the schools and in the youth. Scouting was a perfect medium. Many of the fathers of these boys were miners, ones who were conscious of the millions of tons of iron ore they mined that went to the war effort of World War II. Their jobs in mining and their service in the armed forces complemented one another and promoted an extremely strong sense of pride in their country. They very much wanted their children to carry on these values of hard work and service.

These two young students are here being presented with awards or scholarships by the local American Legion post. The names are missing so it is also reasonable to speculate these were awards to Boys' State and Girls' State. To the left are some of their teachers, presumably ones who were part of the scholarship selection committee. Raising funds for scholarships given to local graduates. Boys' State and Girls' State were mini-conventions that offered opportunities to learn about the role of government in a democracy.

The origin of this picture is uncertain, but it is entirely possible this was taken at the Girl Scout camp on Burntside Lake. The Girl Scout Council was established under the sponsorship of the Rotary Club in 1921. Several troops were organized and many activities begun including summer camp activities. Mrs. Herbert Hoover visited the camp in 1922. One room in the high school was designated as the Girl Scout office and for a time it was staffed by a full time person. During this time, the Girls Athletic Association was also organized and girls were active in several intramural sports such as swimming, basketball, volleyball, track and field, and softball.

Until about 2010, the Duluth newspapers—both daily and Sunday—were delivered to homes by paperboys and papergirls. This picture shows them being feted at a banquet in the Blue Room of the Forest Hotel. This was most likely an event sponsored by one of the local service clubs. The year was 1945 and Betty Markovich Kunstel was the only girl paper carrier.

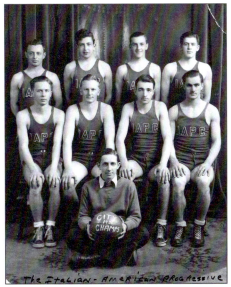

The Italian-American Progressive Club basketball team. Fraternal, ethnic, and other organizations often sponsored sports teams that played games locally with other groups and with still others on the Iron Range.

Another championship team of young men sponsored by the I.O.O.F.—Independent Order of Odd Fellows.

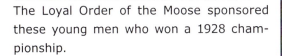

The Loyal Order of the Moose sponsored these young men who won a 1928 championship.

The V.F.W.—Veterans of Foreign Wars—sponsored this baseball team who won a state championship title in 1961.

Some local fraternal and service organizations sponsored athletic teams for the children of their members. Here is a basketball team called the "Kay Jays" who were sponsored by the K.S.K.J., a Slovenian fraternal organization.

Americanization — the Immigrants Become Citizens

A local woman who had graduated from Duluth State Teachers' College, Clara Handberg, began her teaching career in the county school system. Seeing a need for English and basic skills among the immigrants themselves, she began classes in some of their homes in outlying areas. In 1930 the Ely School Board started the Naturalization Citizen Program. Classes were held three nights a week and were organized on three different levels. After learning the basic skills in English, these adult students went on for more advanced English, current events, and spelling. Clara then instructed classes in naturalization, including American history, government, and citizenship. At the end of the year these immigrants, who were still considered aliens, appeared before a judge who questioned them, and then granted certificates for American citizenship. Clara brought more than a thousand such residents to full citizenship in the United States. She taught these classes from 1923 to 1940. In a twist of fate, she married Nick Mineff who was one of her first students.

In the beginning most of the students were men because in those early years wives and children were included when husbands were granted citizenship. A number of the women, especially those who wanted to learn English, elected to attend Americanization classes on their own.

Mine foremen did not necessarily encourage the immigrants to learn much English. Their thought was that mixing different ethnic groups who could only converse with one another in a very limited way discouraged "idle conversation." Ironically, the workers learned much of one another's language.

Born in Ely in 1892, Clara Handberg guided the local immigrants along their path to American citizenship. She began informal classes in rural homes in 1923 and continued this program until 1940.

One of the first Americanization classes is shown here in the Washington auditorium having just been granted their citizenship papers in August 1934.

One of the last formal Americanization classes in December 1960. The couple in the middle, Mr. and Mrs. Uno Vehkalahti, became citizens but later returned to their homeland in Finland.

Marriage wasn't always for the very young.

The wedding of Clara Handberg and Nick Mineff on September 13, 1942. Nick Mineff was in one of Clara's citizenship classes. He was born in Bulgaria and owned a tavern in Ely.

FORM 2204
U. S. DEPARTMENT OF LABOR
NATURALIZATION SERVICE

TRIPLICATE
(To be given to the person making the Declaration.)

No. 723

UNITED STATES OF AMERICA

DECLARATION OF INTENTION

☞ **Invalid for all purposes seven years after the date hereof**

State of Minnesota
County of St. Louis } ss.:

In the _____ District _____ Court
of St. Louis County, Minnesota

I, _____ Fredrik Huovinen _____, aged ____39____ years, occupation ____Miner____, do declare on oath that my personal description is: Color __white__, complexion ____light____, height _5_ feet _8½_ inches, weight __158__ pounds, color of hair __light brown__, color of eyes __blue__ other visible distinctive marks ____None____

I was born in ____Kestila, Finland____ on the ___13th___ day of ____April____, anno Domini 1 890 ; I now reside at ___P. O. Box 664, Ely, Minnesota___
(Give number, street, city or town, and State.)

I emigrated to the United States of America from ____Liverpool, England____ on the vessel ____Virginian to Quebec, Canada____ ; my last
(If the alien arrived otherwise than by vessel, the character of conveyance or name of transportation company should be given)
foreign residence was ____Kestila, Finland____ ; I am _____ married; the name of my {wife/husband} is __Lempi__ ; {she/he} was born at __Ely, Minnesota__ and now resides at ___P. O. Box 664, Ely, Minnesota___

It is my bona fide intention to renounce forever all allegiance and fidelity to any foreign prince, potentate, state, or sovereignty, and particularly to _____ The Republic of Finland _____, of which I am now a citizen

I arrived at the port of ____Sault Ste Marie____, in the State of ____Michigan____, on or about the __2nd.__ day of ____July____, anno Domini 1 910 ; I am not an anarchist; I am not a polygamist nor a believer in the practice of polygamy; and it is my intention in good faith to become a citizen of the United States of America and to permanently reside therein: SO HELP ME GOD.

Fredrik Huovinen
(Original signature of declarant)

[SEAL]

Subscribed and sworn to before me in the office of the Clerk of said Court this _6th_ day of __March__, anno Domini 192 8

J. P. JOHNSON

Clerk of the _____ District _____ Court.

By _O. M. Selin_____, Deputy Clerk.

Ely, Minnesota.

The Declaration of Intention was considered "the first paper" and was followed, sometimes several years later, by "final papers." Fredrik Huovinen became a citizen in 1920, having renounced his Finnish citizenship. Only three years before that Finns were entered as "citizens of Imperial Russia" since Finland had been under Russian domination for nearly 100 years.

U. S. DEPARTMENT OF LABOR
NATURALIZATION SERVICE

ORIGINAL

LIST No. 7

CITIZENSHIP PETITIONS GRANTED

State of Minnesota

County of St. Louis

ss:

In the District Court

of St. Louis County at Ely

Upon consideration of the petitions for citizenship listed below on lines 1 to 30, inclusive, the affidavits in support thereof, and testimony taken in open Court, and the Court having found that each of the petitioners so listed herein intends to reside permanently in the United States, had in all respects complied with the naturalization laws of the United States in each such case applicable, and was entitled to be admitted a citizen, and each of such petitioners having taken the oath of allegiance required by the naturalization laws and regulations, it is hereby ordered that each of such petitioners be, and hereby is, admitted to become a citizen of the United States of America.

LINE NO.	PETITION NO.	NAME OF PETITIONER	CHANGE OF NAME TO
1	663	Anna Elisabeth Hyvarinen	
2	660	Agnes Tekavec Kunstelj	
3	677	Brigita Zitnik Hribar	
4	678	Louis Garni	
5	679	Katarina Zajec Kosmach	
6	680	Evan Elioff	John Elioff
7	681	Sabatino Possansini	
8	682	Ivana Kovac Telich	
9	683	Leopold Annerer	
10	684	Aliina Haanpaa Matikainen	
11	685	Erik Gunnar Ronn	
12	687	Maybelle Reum Herseth	
13	688	Frances Kavicic Mese	
14	689	Katherine Emhilion Apostle	
15	690	Emilia Haanpaa Rosted	
16	691	John Globechnik	
17	692	Harry Rosevear	
18	695	Carl John Severson	
19	697	Helen Hansen Severson	
20	698	George Simonoff	George Simon
21	699	Annie Matelich Janezich	
22	700	Elena Hivanen Kosola	
23	701	Mary Jerich Polynar	
24	702	Aino Koski Rajamaki	
25	703	Milia Korpi Salmi	
26	704	Sanna Ulvinen Ranta	
27	705	Johan Gradisher	
28	706	Alho Hokkanen	
29	707	Fredrik Huovinen	
30	708	Emil Nieminen	Emil Niemi

Prayer granted for change of name in petitions No 680, 698, 708.

By the Court, this 15th day of July, 19 31

Edward Freeman

Judge.

This document from 1931 grants American citizenship to 30 Ely residents. Number 29 is Fredrik Huovinen is the same person who filed his first papers ten years before. Note that two men appear to also be using more Americanized versions of their names. The list indicates mix of Yugoslavians, Finns, a Greek, and other nationalities.

1898
ELY MEN IN SPANISH-AMERICAN WAR
1. Oscar Kauppi   2. Oscar Hakko   3. Johns Harri   4. Chris Saari   5. Frank Ruper   6. Phillip Sheridan   7. Jacob Maki

When the call to arms for the Spanish-American War was sounded,
these forty-two men responded.

One of my most vivid recollections is joining a crowd of towns-people who had gathered at the station to send off the Ely men going off to World War I. The train left about 12:30 or 1 p.m. and once I remember I rushed down to the station with a dish towel still in my hand; I had been drying the noon dinner dishes. To us kids, all the men going off to war were heroes.

-From a letter by Mrs. John B. (Corinne L.) Olli
February 15th, 1975

During WW I many young men enlisted in the service. By the time of WW II, some miners were exempted because the mining of iron ore was necessary for the war effort. Ely by then had the highest per capita number of men in service than anywhere else in the entire country.

Frank Lozar was the first Elyite killed in WW I. The first American Legion Post was named in this honor. When his body was returned to Ely, a huge funeral was held at the Catholic church and a funeral parade marched from the church to the cemetery. His mother was sent black mourning clothes to wear for the funeral and her period of grieving. The local legion post was first named the Frank Lozar American Legion Post.

Matt Banks served in the US Army during WW I. Note the heavy woolen uniforms that were worn at that time.

The end of WW I required a parade such as the town had never seen previously. The men in white shirts, ties, suits and hats were perhaps businessmen. The present Ace Hardware building was then Berglund Bros. store and the present Wells Fargo Bank was then much smaller and called the First National Bank of Ely.

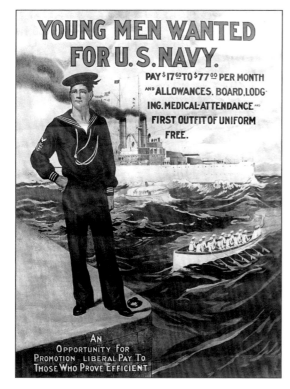

World War I Navy recruitment and Red Cross donation solicitation posters.

Sgt. 1Cl Arthur J. Duggan came to Ely as a surveyor with the US Geological Survey in the years before WW I. Although from the East, he claimed Ely as his home. He died of nerve gassing in France and is buried in the St. Mihiel American Cemetery in Garches, France at the request of his mother.

A parade on Memorial Day in 1922 to the cemetery from the old entrance on Highway 1. This custom began after World War I ended in 1918.

THE MINES

In winter and in summer miners grind
Beneath the surface where the iron lies,
With tiny shining lamps to help them find
The ore. While up and down the shaft there flies
A busy skip that totes rich loads of ore
From pockets down below, to fat stock piles.
Enormous hills are formed that shrink before
The huge machines that load the miles and miles
Of ore cars rolling down long endless tracks.
They lead out into cities far and near
For vital industries. A miner lacks
Privation, miseries and any fear
Of insecurity, for now the times
Are pressing needs; and ore is in our mines.

by Nancy King from *Yes, Really It's Ely* by Ruth King

This piece depicts the mines when they were in full production during WW II.

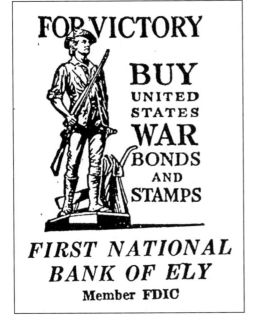

Albin Mrace (left) and William Loushin (right) were both killed on December 7, 1941, in the Japanese attack on Pearl Harbor. William Loushin was onboard the USS Arizona and Albin Mrace was onboard the USS West Virginia. After WW II the local American Legion was renamed the Lozar-Mrace-Loushin Post.

Steve Grahek, Seaman First Class/US Coast Guard, received a number of honors including the Bronze and Silver Stars.

Frank Jershe, son of Slovenian immigrants, served in the military police.

Arthur Garni, son of Italian immigrants, served in the USN in WW II.

One of the many Ely men who enlisted in WW II—the War interrupted their lives for an extended time but the men had a real sense of duty and patriotism. Joseph F. Sheryak, son of Yugoslavian immigrants, served in the USAF.

Joseph Garni served honorably in the USN during WW II and operated and then sold his tavern business to Anton Zaverl. He was the brother of Arthur Garni who also served in the USN.

About seventy Ely women responded to the call for volunteers. Two were known to have enlisted and gone to boot camp in Iowa, one serving time in a payroll division (Katherine Buccowich) and the other (Clarice Kobe) who went to radio and television school.

PVT. MARGARET E. LAMBERT, 312 East Conan street, Ely, "brand new" Air-WAC, gives a crisp salute. (As yet she has not received her insignia.)

An article about First Lt. Katherine Skradski.

Margaret Lambert, Air-WAC

Lt. Skradski Is First Nurse to Receive Air Medal in Pacific

First Lt. Katherine Skradski

Ely, Minnesota — First Lt. Katherine Skradski, member of Lodge No. 114, AFU, received the first Air Medal awarded to a nurse in the Pacific theater, according to dispatches received from the Pacific headquarters of the medical air evacuation squadron. The citation accompanying the medal stated that Lieutenant Skradski participated in numerous long, overwater flights, returning battle casualties to base hospitals in rear areas.

Lieut. Katherine Skradski is the daughter of Mr. and Mrs. Peter Skradski, Sr. of Ely, Minn. Nine members of this family are all AFU members and the father, Peter Skradski, Sr. is one of our most active members. The Lieutenant has several brothers also serving in the armed forces.

Congratulations to Lt. Skradski on being the first of all nurses in the Pacific theater of war to be awarded the Air Medal!

Here half of the 300 men serving in World War II are pictured here in the store window of Johnny "Bucca's" City Meat and Grocery Store. Ely had one of the highest per capita enrollment in the nation—more than 1500 men and women served from 1940-1945, which was nearly twenty-five percent of the population.. Fifty-two (or more) died in the War. At the end of the war people literally danced in the streets. Veteran Tauno Maki wrote: "Now that victory is won, and these boys sleep under the waves, in greening fields, under shell-shattered palms, beneath the sands of desolate wastes. They sleep peacefully, for they know they have done well. The sleep confidently, in the expectation that their sacrifice was of incalculable benefit to the loves ones they left behind."

ELY RED CROSS

The Ely Red Cross is very active in war work. In all there are 5 groups totaling 70 sewers. Since August over 500 garments such as dresses, pajamas, nightgowns, infants dresses, boys shirts, overalls, etc., were made up and sent forward. Mrs. William Jones is in charge of the sewing group. Left to right Mrs. Emil Norby, Mrs. Frank Schweiger, Mrs. Matt Martin, Mrs. Harry Homer directly behind Mrs. Frank Schweiger, Mrs. Walter D. Carlson, Mrs. John Wilmunen, Mrs. Frank Carlson, Mrs. H. N. Sutherland, Mrs. E. Merrill; standing, Mrs. W. J. Leod, back row left to right, H. C. Newgord, Mrs. Will Niemi, Mrs. E. Siro, Mrs. J. Marshall, Mrs. J. W. Shaw, Mrs. Densmore. There are separate groups of knitters.

The war effort during WW II also involved those who did not serve in the military. Here is one of the local Ely Red Cross sewing groups There were five such groups with more than seventy sewers. They made all garments of all kinds. There also were separate groups of who knit items for servicemen.

During the war years such materials as aluminum and tin were collected to be recycled for the war effort. This picture from 1943 shows some well-known early Ely men. On the left is Art Knutson, who was a long-time city clerk and who was considered to be "Mr. Ely History" for many decades. To his right is Grant McMahan, local businessman, county commissioner, and from whom Grant McMahan Boulevard was named. Douglas Nankervis, on the right, was the chief of police.

During the Korean Conflict, local women volunteered to serve as plane spotters for enemy planes that might be flying over the town, possibly from over the Canadian border. It was thought Ely was vulnerable because of the iron mines here that were producing the ore for the steel that supplied the "war machine."

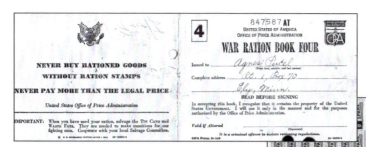

As early as 1918 women were working in war plants, making meals without meat and sometimes wheat. School children filled Liberty Books (later called Defense Stamps) with ten and twenty cent stamps. When they were filled they were converted into War Bonds. This effort continued during WW II and even into the 1950s, all to help pay down the war debt.

A "Disney" certificate for a war bond, 1945.

Mr. and Mrs. Joseph Sheryak (women's names often not mentioned) shown at their wartime wedding in the 1940s. It was a difficult time for young couples when the prospective husband went off to war. Many was the time the couple would be married during the soldier's leave.

Three Mrace brothers gave the "ultimate sacrifice) in WW II, all in different European battles. They were Albin, Anton, and Frank Mrace and a funeral for all three was held at St. Anthony's Catholic Church on July 14, 1948. At least several thousand people turned out for the funeral and the procession to the cemetery.

The discharge certificate shows military record data for POPESH JOSEPH L.

Most WW II veterans returned home to Ely after the War ended and found employment in the mines. Among them was Frank Popesh, whose Honorable Discharge certificate is shown here.

From One 'Buddy' to Another--

"Welcome Home"

Back to God's Country!

There's No Place Like in the Whole Wide World. There is No Emotion Stronger Than the Joy of Coming Home.

Yes, "Buddy", We've Been Waiting for You — We Need You to Help us Preserve the Victory You Fought to Win.

WW II veterans marching in parade down Sheridan Street. Veterans were always held in the highest regard in Ely—defending the freedom of this country was a long-standing tradition going back to the immigrant generation.

This parade picture shows evidence of a few *servicewomen*.

The Veterans of Foreign Wars and American Legion service groups have overseen the graves of veterans at the Ely Cemetery. Two special plots have been set aside for use by veterans. On Memorial Day the groups arrange for and honor roll program and the placing of flags on graves of veterans throughout the cemetery. In this photo from the 1950s they have gathered for a remembrance of Veterans' Day.

Since WW II, those who have given their lives in wartime have been honored by the service organizations with a wreath at the memorial marker at the City Hall. The women's groups sell poppies to the public. A remembrance service is held at the cemetery on Memorial Day. There is always a large turnout. The memorial marker at the city hall has now been enlarged to include fallen veterans from WW I, WW II, the Korean Conflict, the Vietnam War, and the Persian Gulf War.

Veterans belonging to both the American Legion and the Veterans of Foreign Wars have marched in local parades for many years. Now because of their ages, they ride on a large flatbed truck for the Fourth of July parade.

Veterans' organizations such as the American Legion provided a way for veterans to connect with one another and for them to share some camaraderie. They also helped in their own way to remind the public of the service these men had done in defending our country.

Ely gained a regional reputation with the Drum and Bugle Corps under the direction of Drum Major Harold Dillon, who held the group to very high standards. They were Minnesota State Champions in the early 1930s. There was a tremendous amount of pride in Ely and all the activities that grew out of those years. Nearly the whole town turned out for any parade or special appearance by groups such as this.

Music of all kinds—bands, orchestras, and choirs of all kinds and in the schools, churches, and family gatherings—was very important to the miners and their families.

The Ely Community Band is pictured in front of the Washington School with director Mr. Reinshagen in 1926.

Although this group was organized for a Grape Festival, these singers were a part of the Slovenian Choir that lasted until the early 2000s. On the right is the director, Mary Hutar. She directed the choir for several years and also was the organist at St. Anthony's Catholic Church. She also served as organist from time to time at the Presbyterian church.

While the accordion is a part of many cultures, it was a particular favorite of the Slovenians. Accordions were a part of wedding dances, backyard parties, and live music in local bars. This picture is probably from the 1940s and is particularly interesting because of the African American man who seemed well accepted by the others. Mayor Ernie Hanson has his hand on the man's shoulder.

The Ely Theater opened in 1936 and replaced the old Elco theater one block west on Chapman St. It seated 900 people and was often filled to capacity on weekends for double features and matinees. It was known as the Baehr Building and housed the movie theater, professional offices, and apartments. Before television movie theaters were not only places of entertainment but also for social gatherings.

In the same year, 1936, the State Theater opened in Ely. It too replaced an earlier movie theater in what had been known at one time as the Opera House and is now the Ely Bowling Center. Both theaters are now closed.

Built in 1895 by the Finnish Vesi Temperance Society (see page 10) as a public venue for lectures, musicals, and other programs, this building became known as Ely's Opera House. When membership in the Temperance Society waned, the building was a venue for traveling vaudeville and magic shows in addition to other musical events. From these it became a silent movie theater, a "talkies" theater, and eventually the Ely Bowling Center and Lounge.

The First National Bank of Ely sponsored a bowling team for adult men. This team also won a championship in its "major league."

Slovenians were particularly fond of pig roasts in the summer as part of family gatherings and other celebrations. This one took place on the shore of White Iron Lake, but no one is identified.

Throughout a large part of the mining era there were as many as thirty-one bars in this town that never quite reached 6,000 in population. On Saturday nights these establishments were jammed. There very often was live music and dancing, providing a social outlet after a long hard week working underground.

The keyboard and button box accordions were ever-present in any celebration, be it a Fourth of July parade, wedding reception, or backyard family gathering. More prevalent among the Slovenians and Croatians, there were also some among the Finns.

Now one of the last known public saunas operating in the country, the Ely Steam Bath was built by a Finnish immigrant, Emil Ahola, in 1915. The cement blocks of the original part of the building where hand crafted by him. It features a men's sauna, a women's sauna, and several private saunas. It first catered to the single Finnish immigrants, then to Ely families and individuals of other ethnic backgrounds, and now has become popular among the tourists and canoeists. For a large part of Ely's history it was just a part of the week's agenda to "go to Ahola's sauna" at least on Saturday nights for many of the locals. It was operated by three generations of the Ahola family during most of the town's mining era but is currently operated by the Petrzilka family.

This is a large group of Slovenians at an unknown celebration at an upstairs hall. The inscription indicates that the honorees or hosts are Marco and Madeleine Slogar.

The Oliver Iron Mining Co. owned the point of land called Sandy Point on Shagawa Lake, just north of the mines. Miners were permitted to use it as a recreation spot. A pavilion was built (and later moved to Semer's Park) and a large pier was constructed for swimming and fishing. Family and group picnics were held here, as well as summer conventions for fraternal groups. As the years went on and the facility began to need some fairly extensive repairs, the company closed the park. It contended the park and beach were too much of a liability. The City of Ely then opened Semer's Park.

As a gesture to replace the deteriorating Sandy Point that had been built as a park by the Oliver iron Mining Company, in 1916 Mr. John Semer of Escanaba, MI, donated lakeshore property on Shagawa lake for a public park. The stone buildings, fireplaces, bridges to the two islands, and fire circle were built as a Works Progress Administration or WPA project during the Depression. One of the stone buildings had lavatory facilities and a changing area. The other was a dining pavilion with cooking facilities. The pavilion building that originally stood at Sandy Point was moved to what became known as Semer's Park in 1945. It underwent a complete renovation in the 1980s. A bath house that was added in 1955 and later rebuilt in 1980. A lifeguard is on duty for the swimming area for much of the summer.

Children of all ages have especially enjoyed the beach at Semer's Park for many decades.

The Whitesides, who were prospectors, lumbermen, and developers of the area, donated the area bounded by Sheridan St. and south of Harvey St. and from Seventh to Eighth Ave. E. for a public park. This was in the first years of the 1900s. It became the scene of many activities; flower gardens, a children's playground, and picnic areas, and it

now includes a log band shell, pavilion, and lavatory buildings. Fourth of July events, the Blueberry and Harvest Moon Festivals, the winter snow sculptures, city band concerts, and numerous other activities are now held here.

The park is home to swings, sandboxes, monkey bars, sandboxes, picnic tables, and flower gardens among other things. These boys are quite happy with the slide.

While there are still parades on the Fourth of July and food, games, and fun in the park, another July Festival has become hugely popular. The main activities are in Whiteside Park and consist of arts and crafts booths, lots of food, and much fun. Approximately 30,000 people come to town during this three day festival the last weekend in July.

The lakes and woods bordering the town came to be regarded as the "back yard" of Elyites young and old. These young women and what appears to be a young man perhaps acting as some kind of guide, are enjoying the best of a summer day.

As can be seen from this picture, canoe trips into the wilderness were a part of Ely from rather early times. Note the wooden spoke wheels on the caravan and the Duluth packs in the lower right corner.

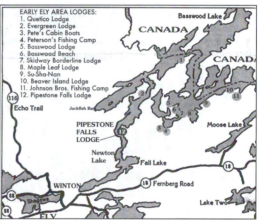

A map of the early Ely area lodges.

There were several means of reaching the resorts that once dotted such lakes as Basswood Lake. It was a roadless area so tourist came in by canoe, motor launch, airplanes, for a brief time with pack horses, and with a unique vehicle/ vessel called a "duck." "Ducks" were equipped both with wheels for land travel and with propellers for traveling across water. They were first used in military operations in WW II and were called amphibians.

The Ely area abounded in lakes that provided kids with a place to swim. Many, many families had summer cabins on nearby lakes where the children came to enjoy swimming, boating, canoeing, taking saunas, and just being in the "woods."

Brothers Andy and Frank Tout-loff, who both were of Chippewa or Ojibwe heritage and from this area, worked in underground mining in Ely. Andy's son Roger also worked in the mine, presumably during the years he went to Ely Junior College. He was an outstanding basketball player in high school and junior col-

lege and went on to become a teacher in Chisholm, MN. Andy and Frank both were also well known wilderness guides.

The Superior National Forest, of which the Boundary Waters Canoe Area is a part, was established by legislation instigated by President Theodore Roosevelt in 1909. Since that time the U.S. Forest Service has had an impact on the economy of Ely. Fighting forest fires has been a big part of what the Forest Service has done and this picture from 1916 shows forestry crew stringing telephone lines in the area.

Marie Sarkipato, daughter of Finnish immigrants, was not only a state champion in girls' swimming but she became well-known as the first wilderness girl guide in the country. She was featured on the cover of several sporting magazines and while still in high school guided tourists on canoe trips in the wilderness.

The period beginning in the 1950s and continuing on into the 1960s was a contentious time in Ely. The advocates of creating a pristine wilderness area were pitted against those who saw logging, resorts, fly-in fish camps, and motor boats (and in the winter, snowmobiles) as a positive recreational opportunities. The noted author Sigurd Olson and several politicians were hung in effigy on the streets of Ely.

Logging was a real economic factor in town and loggers were affected by the wilderness legislation as much as those with recreational interests.

Not only was fishing a part of many lives, so was winter ice fishing. The Chamber of Commerce sponsored fishing contests in February in the 1950s for a number of years. Hundreds, and even several thousand people turned out. Some were of course contestants and others were spectators. Concessions of all kinds were sold and the event took on a carnival-like atmosphere.

Kaleva Bay Lodge, constructed of local pine logs by the Knights of Kaleva, on Burntside Lake was also the scene of winter festivities, this one named the Trout-a-Rama fishing contest. Roads were plowed on the lake and hundreds of cars, fishermen, and spectators vied for various prizes given for winning catches of the day. The crowds were fed and entertained in the main lodge on shore. The fishing contest was discontinued several years later after several years of unstable ice conditions on the lake. Four local men with their catches of the day during a Trout-a-Rama fishing contest in the 1960s.

Shown here are Frank Loushin and Luke Skantz with their "winners" during the contest in 1966.

Sled dog races that ran right through town were popular in the 1970s. A film was even shot one year with Ely as an Alaska town for the Iditarod race. In the middle of this picture is the State Theater, one of two rather large movie houses in town. Both are now closed.

While snowshoeing was and is a form of winter recreation, it was also a means of getting around in the woods for other reasons such as hunting, winter fishing, and trapping.

In the early years of Ely, hunting was not only a sport but also a necessity to provide meat for families, especially during the lean years of work. Poaching was commonplace in spite of the efforts of the conservation officers. Deer hunting remained a popular sport throughout the more prosperous years. This picture, probably from the early 1960s shows a group of men back from a particularly good hunt.

Two women getting ready to go out trekking on snowshoes. Of course in those days Ely had winters with much more snow than in the 2000s.

Winter in Ely is a magical time for kids. "Big Dutch" on the golf course was great for toboggans, sleds of all kinds, and beginning skiers. Other sliding hills were Conan Street down from the Lincoln School, Boundary Street, and the schoolyard. This was before the era of more sophisticated skis, snow mobiles, and ATVs. These two children are simply having fun sledding down a city street.

For many years Santa Claus' stand-in was Dan Toms. He appeared with small gifts or candy for the children at various fraternal organizations, the Community Center, and the school. A family with six young boys lived across the alley from Mr. Toms' home and the boys just could not understand why Santa made so many trips to the Toms' house when there were only two children there.

This young fisherman seems well equipped to win a prize catch.

Snow still on the ground and the opening a fishing season likely a whole month away, this young man is practicing to be one of the first to wet a line.

Parades were not uncommon even in the winter. Up through the 1950s horses, sleighs, and elaborate floats were a part of it all. It is interesting to note the heavy woolen winter clothing worn by those on the right—a far cry from today's Polartec, down, fleece, and Spandex outerwear.

A tug-of-war contest on First Avenue East for Fourth of July in 1924 – the brick building in the background was then Berglund Bros. hardware and general merchandise. It is now Merhar's Ace Hardware.

Children, costumes, and flags—all a part of the Fourth of July parade.

Costumes were almost mandatory for the Fourth of July, at least for the children, but many of the adults got into the spirit of things as well.

Children, some happy and some not, dressed up for the Fourth. The building in the background was then the Rothman Garage and is now the Senior Citizen Center.

For a number of years, primarily in the 1940s after WW II and into the 1950s, the Chamber of Commerce sponsored "Roaring Stoney Days." Men were cajoled into growing beards, parades and other celebrations were held, and the locals really got into the spirit. The Stoney River, north and east of Ely, was one of the waterways used to transport logs to the saw mills in Winton from the 1880s until the 1920s. The lumberjacks were often rough but colorful characters. This picture was taken at the Sportsman's Inn (now home of Wintergreen, Inc.) which was owned by the jovial Joe Klun. He is shown here as the "sheriff' of the celebration activities.

Roaring Stoney Days gave a special atmosphere to the Fourth of July celebrations for many years. They used as a theme the logging days of Ely's early history—this one from July Fourth of 1948.

Particularly during the Roaring Stoney celebrations, there were parades with impressive floats, a King and Queen Ely, and numerous bands. Several, such as the high school band, the city band, and the Drum and Bugle Corps, were from Ely, but others also came from other Range communities. In the 1950s and 1960s the prosperity of the town was much in evidence.

Clarence Lundberg and Ed Stenke entered the beard growing contest held by Roaring Stoney Days in 1948. Ed was very involved with that year's celebration and walked around town wielding a shillelagh.

Kids march past Vertin's Café in 3rd of July Parade 1976. Note boy carrying BWCA protest sign. Parade was combination Bi-Centennial and All Class Reunion event.

Choosing royalty for the Fourth of July continued on well into the 1950s. In this undated picture Dr. J. P. Grahek, a local medical doctor and long-term mayor was King Ely.

The Memorial High School band was the pride of Ely and for years regularly appeared in Fourth of July parades in town and on the Range. They also appeared in other special parades and in concerts.

101

Nat Dargontina and Elvira Colombo were married at St. Anthony's church on August 21, 1929. It was a typical large Italian wedding. The Italian population in Ely was not so very large and a number of those present in the picture came from other nearby Range communities. Other nationalities are represented here as well. Little did the couple know what would be facing them in October of that year when the stock market crashed, the mines closed (at least for a time), and unemployment was widespread. Their son Ronald did receive a college education and became a teacher.

Growing and Harvesting in Ely

Farming around Ely was mostly subsistence farming. Families grew enough for their own needs and perhaps enough eggs, milk, produce, and meat to sell for extra income. The Slovenians were especially skilled gardeners growing vegetables and fruits to feed the large families of the time. Mrs. Frank Sasek is shown in her garden in 1915. It was located near the corner of Fourth Ave. E. and Sheridan St.

Presumably this was a garden in Chandler location but it is otherwise unidentified. Note the pole bean on the upper right and the cucumbers in the lower left. The cluster of buildings, although not a farm, is somehow reminiscent of rural Europe.

The Partti farm. Finnish men were among the first to leave the underground mines and to look for land to start a small farm, but it was a tough living at best.

Bill Hanson was a Minnesota State Game, Fish, and Wildlife Warden headquartered out of the district ranger office in Winton. He was known as a fair and just man and a friend to both white man and Indian. In this picture he is visiting with Mrs. Chosa at Basswood Lake as she is preparing the bounty from the wild rice harvest.

Families worked together in gardens and on the small farms. Potatoes grew rather well in the sometimes poor rocky soil and in the short growing season. They were a staple for the immigrant families, both those from northern and southern Europe.

For most of the mining era, Ely was a paternalistic society, no doubt a reflection of the ethnic heritage of the population and the times. The women and wives, were responsible for more than we can imagine today—raising families, running households, tending large gardens, sewing clothes, serving on committees, in groups, and in churches to provide for the "betterment" of the community. Occasionally some of them found time to enjoy a few recreational activities outside their homes.

For many years women depended heavily on their children for help with the heavy burdens they themselves faced every day. The families were often quite large and there were large meals, gardening, cleaning, and laundering to deal with. Boys and girls alike helped out their mothers. It is quite true that there was no real sex education in most homes and what the young learned came from their friends. Religion, often connected to ethnicity, was a most important factor for marriage. This unspoken "rule" lasted until the 1950s at least.

Women who did work mostly worked in the home by taking in sewing or boarders. Some even took in washing. A few women did work outside the home as teachers, nurses, midwives, child care, or as cleaning women. This was certainly true during the Depression years. Educating their children was a goal of many women. The local schools, especially the junior college, made that dream rather accessible. Such social problems as incest and domestic abuse were not rare but never talked about. Women did wear pants much earlier and more often than is commonly thought, but seldom if ever in public.

The first petit jury of the District Court in Minnesota to have women serve as jurors was on July 12, 1921, in Ely, Minnesota. Included among them were Mrs. Laura Lockhart, Mrs. Caroline Quigley, and Mrs. Alice Miller.

The first petit jury of the District Court in Minnesota to have women as jurors.
Ely, Minnesota, July 12th 1921.
TOP-Right to left: John H.Clow, Charles E.Bauglet, J.B.Zweifel, A.J.Butchart, Joseph Grams
Louis McCullough----BOTTOM: Mrs.Laura Lockhart, Mrs.Caroline Quigley, Mrs.Alice Miller,
Fred C. Harris, K.E.Violette, John B.Seglem.   J.A.Hole was Deputy Sheriff in charge of

Mrs. Sophia Koski was widowed at a young age and left with a large family. She took in boarders to make ends meet. She is shown here with her daughter Helia who became a teacher in the Lincoln School. Sophia lived to be over 100 years of age. Like many of the immigrants of the time, she "got by" her entire life without knowing much English, but she read Finnish newspapers and books "by the barrel."

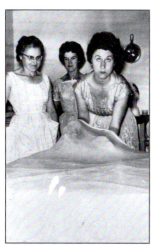

For many years women were not often identified by their own first names. Here are pictured Mrs. Kidd, Mrs. Hutar, and Mrs. Feroni making very large (and very thin) potica dough.

The Finn Hill Gang in 1920 – There were many Saari children, several Nappas, one Sipola (all Finns) and one Fallmaeir girl (not Finnish). Finn Hill was really one of the first mining locations just west of the Chandler mine and many Finnish immigrants chose to settle there.

Bonnie Maddern, Donna Hokkanen, Patsy Maddern, Rita Kylmala, and a dog on Finn Hill in the 1930s

Helmi Autio, Inez Lampi, and Sara Mitchell enjoying ice cream on a summer day.

Two young Elyites perhaps out "politicking" in 1946.

Four young friends in 1925.

Clearly this happy boy senses no hardships of the early years in Ely.

This picture seems to be three generations of the Chinn family who lived on Harvey Street. One of the Mr. Chinn's in Ely was a mining captain. The family came originally from England.

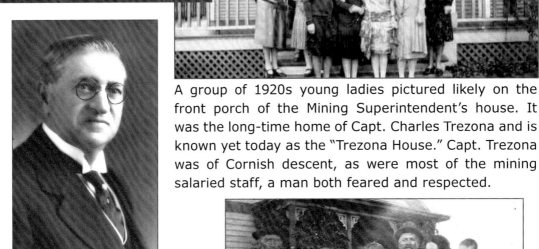

A group of 1920s young ladies pictured likely on the front porch of the Mining Superintendent's house. It was the long-time home of Capt. Charles Trezona and is known yet today as the "Trezona House." Capt. Trezona was of Cornish descent, as were most of the mining salaried staff, a man both feared and respected.

A formal portrait of Capt. Charles Trezona.

The last names of these people, Carlberg, Anderson, Larson, and Lindbeck tells us this is one of the Swedish families in Ely. The date is probably one from the 1920s.

Alex Sansted Family. The family name is actually of Swedish origin, as was the case for a number of Finnish families. Finland was a province of Sweden for more than 600 years until 1809. The Finns came, along with other immigrants, to the Ely area seeking employment and cheap land. In the process they discovered the wonderful educational opportunities that were available to their children.

This would be a typical family portrait of a Finnish mining family – dated 1926. The back indicates this was a postcard used to send New Year's greetings (in Finnish). Many families did not have a telephone and sent post cards the same way we now send emails even to local friends and family.

The Moses Hokkanen family (and most definitely Finnish).

Four unidentified young men— the style of the high leather boots indicates they were probably of Finnish background.

This group of people, although unidentified, is of southern European background. The costumes of the women and the accordion player suggest their heritage is Slovenian.

The dress, demeanor, and architectural details of the house in the background suggest the man is perhaps a businessman and not likely a miner. He may have been Slovenian or Scandinavian but more likely he was English.

The Mustar wedding. Weddings, especially among the Slovenians and Southern Europeans, were big events that often lasted for several days. Notice the bride's elaborate head piece, the accordion player, and all the very well dressed family and friends.

Gust A. Maki came to Ely from Finland at the age of eight years old .His father, who had a shoe and leather goods shop, died when Gust was twelve. Gust left school to work in the blacksmith shop of the Chandler mine, later became a retail clerk, and finally established his own men's clothing store. Senja came to Ely from southern Minnesota when she was seventeen. They met walking along the railroad tracks near the depot and were married in the Temperance Hall, also known as the Opera Hall, on May 1, 1907.

The couple is unidentified but the photographer, Charles "Charlie" Hendrickson, is noteworthy since he had first been a miner and then later established his own photo studio in Ely.

The wedding of Pat Sayovitz and Harold Koski was the first wedding in new St. Anthony's Catholic church on June 14, 1958. The church had been dedicated only one week before.

Anniversary picture of John Glavan and his wife. Mr. Glavan was a miner all his working life as were a number of his family. They were Slovenian.

Funerals, at least in the frontier days of this town, were often big events. The funeral coaches—horse drawn— were quite elaborate with large glass windows on three sides. It is not known whether the "Millicent" written on the picture is the little girl on the board sidewalk or the name of the deceased. The picture is from Winton.

The name of the deceased is not given but many others such as Sayovitz, Glavan, Hutar, Slogar, Kunstelj, Erchul, Bolka, and Mertel tell that this is a Slovenian funeral. It was common in the early 1900s to have a wake at the family home.

The wake for Mary Pluth who died at the age of 51 in 1916, was held at the Pluth's place of business on Sheridan Street. The young boy is Steve Pluth who was twelve years old at the time. Also pictured are the husband and the other sons and daughters.

Indians built spirit houses out of twigs and branches and later lumber over the graves of the dead. Such was the case on Indian Island in Burntside Lake. An opening near the top of each gable allowed the spirits to depart and return. This picture shows another burial ground on Basswood Lake.

A rather elegant funeral coach reminiscent of those seen in continental Europe in the 1800s or early 1900s. The names Tulla, Pietila, and Kaasalainen as pall bearers indicate this as a Finnish funeral.

109

During the 1918-1919 flu epidemic many people, especially younger ones, perished. Even entire families succumbed and thus double, triple, and even more victims were buried at the same time. The ribbons on the mourners represent lodges.

Grave of early settler Isaac Rova. The old cemetery near the present golf course was found to be on private land. One of the landowners was a Smuk family (apparently not related to the present Smuk family in Ely). The Smuk farm name carried with it some irony—"Smoke's Farm." Some of the local old-timers, at least those in the barbershops, bars, and coffee shops began referring to the new cemetery as "Smoke's Farm."

Immigrants came to American and this area lured by the prospect of ready jobs in the mines, inexpensive land (and the opportunity to have their own home), and the mobility that was available for their children with the opportunity of a free public education. Shown here are Joseph Mismash and John Jurisich in front of a pre-WW II home on East Chapman St.

Two Finnish girls outside the first school building in Ely. The building in the background is a laundry run by a Chinese immigrant. He had left Ely by the 1930s.

These young ladies were very likely connected with the Burntside Lake Girl Scout camp.

Grandma Tabaki was a familiar face as was that of her dog Trouble.

The Boshey family lived on reservation land on Lake Vermilion but spent their summers on an island in Burntside Lake that was reserved for their use by mining baron Martin Pattison. Although the Bosheys and perhaps other Indians had used this island as a summer camp for many years, it was after Joe Boshey

rescued Mr. Pattison when his canoe overturned and saved him from drowning that the Bosheys were given the legal right to use the island for many years. The band now owns the island where there is a burial ground. Joe Boshey was a chief of his band.

One of Ely's more dynamic women came with the name of Mary Catherine Brown. She and her husband Allen were well-known for their years of operating the Paul Bunyan Shop on the portage on Basswood Lake. Mary's involvement extended to life in Ely in the form of Girl Scouts, St. Mary's Episcopal Church, Northern Lakes Arts Association, community theater, Music and Drama Club, and other civic endeavors.

One of the Gawboy children was Carl. He obtained a degree in art and eventually became a college art professor. Beyond that he became a well known artist who painted mostly rural scenes of both Native Americans and locals, often Finns. Scenes with brilliant colors in the skies are one of his trademarks. He also began the Bois Forte Gallery in Ely.

Helmi Jarvinen went as a young woman to teach school on the Indian reservation. During her time there she met Robert Gawboy and they later married and settled on Helmi's parents homestead near Birch Lake. They had a large family, all of whom had a college education and successful careers. The family knew both Indian and Finnish traditions and here is shown along with some of their wild rice harvest in a beautiful birch bark basket. Note Mr. Gawboy reading a book, quite probably to Mrs. Gawboy.

LOOKING IN THE REAR VIEW MIRROR

◈ ◈ ◈

Underground mining came to a sudden and complete end on April Fool's Day of 1967.

Looking back, it seems incredible that no one had foreseen this. Only ten years before and again five years later—Ely had experienced building "booms." No one saw the shadow looming on the horizon. One wonders if anyone at all suspected mining was nearing its end—especially mining company officials. If they did have such knowledge it was never shared.

During 1956-57 millions of dollars went into new construction: a new Kennedy Elementary School, Ely-Bloomenson Community Hospital, the Baptist and St. Anthony's Catholic churches, and the Jugoslav National Home/JCPenney building. New homes sprung on the east side of town. Northwest Bank (later Wells-Fargo) expanded its building. And, the taconite mine in Babbitt further buoyed up the optimism the town was experiencing.

In 1962 things were still on a roll. The expenditures were not in the millions of dollars this time but were nonetheless substantial. Ray, Leo, and Norman Kainz moved their sawmill operation from Sawbill Landing on the North Shore to Ely, and they promised to provide forty new jobs. The Forest Chevrolet Co. doubled its garage and showroom space. The local Masonic lodge built a large two story building on Chapman Street, housing the local telephone company on the ground level. Anderson Produce increased their production from 7,000 to 14,000 eggs per day with an expanded building. On South Central Avenue the Ely Cooperative Association completed a modern food market.

And then—just five years later—the booms became a bust. The last underground mine, the Pioneer, closed without warning. Some miners were entitled to early retirement, some went to work in the taconite plants in Mountain Iron or Babbitt and others found lesser paying jobs locally. Many had no choice but to move elsewhere. A whole generation of younger people left and never returned. The population of Ely became noticeably gray.

The end had come like a thief in the night. The underground mining that had been the economic lifeblood of the town drained away.

As people left and businesses closed, the population of the town shrank to almost half of its once more than six thousand inhabitants. Student numbers shrank accordingly. Of the people who did remain many were those who had experienced two World Wars and the Great Depression. These were the hardy, self-reliant souls who had planted big gardens; canned fruits, vegetables, and venison; had stored bent nails in coffee cans; and had saved aluminum foil, newspapers, and tin cans for the war effort. They had cherished hunting, fishing, taking saunas at their cabins, and the camaraderie of the town. Along the way they somehow braided together a culture of different strands and hues.

Simon Bourgin was a native son who became a well-known journalist. He observed on several occasions that Ely has survived because it had a unique ability to reinvent itself. Perhaps it will do so again. All that remains of those miners and the five underground mines now are the morning mists that rise like ghosts over the now water-filled cavity called Miner's Lake.

—David Kess

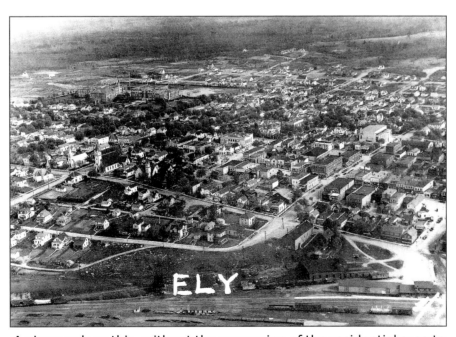

A view such as this, without the expansion of the residential area to the south and east and with the mining activity in the foreground, is probably from the late 1930s or early 1940s.

MINING DEATHS

In those early years the newspaper accounts of their deaths often stated "single with relatives back in the old country." Many of the men were in their early twenties. As the decades passed, more miners were local men with families who lived here. By the 1950s, many of the men were over 50 years of age, and it is not unusual to read that a miner dropped dead of a heart attack on the job.

The miners whose deaths are listed worked in the Chandler, Savoy, Sibley, Pioneer, Zenith, Section Thirty southeast of Ely, and the Mud Creek Mine, under several owners and names, west of Ely.

The project to identify miners who had died was initiated by Judy Swenson when she was Director of the EWHS from July 2000 to April 2005. The purpose in listing the deaths of those who died is to acknowledge their identity and honor their contribution to a town's history. The process we used to identify the miners who died involved searching and cross referencing a number of sources:

-newspapers on file in the Ely Winton Historical Society which date back to the
   very beginning of mining in Ely
-death records on file at the Ely City Hall (which are available starting in 1895
   after mining had begun)
-church records (with thanks to Mary Ann Lekatz for her search of Saint
   Anthony's Church records)
-Minnesota Mining Deaths from 1889 - 1900 by Stina B. Green
-limited available Mining Inspectors Reports on file at the Minnesota Discovery
   Center in Chisholm
-records from the Ely cemetery

With so many inconsistencies in records, names may have been missed or records misinterpreted. In some cases records did not agree. We tried to find at least two records that agreed for each miner. In a few cases this was not possible because newspapers were missing for a particular date or there were no extant death records. Names were incongruent. For instances, the newspaper might print the Americanized name while the death record might show the birth name from the country where the miner was born.

Following the list of miners who died in mining accidents in Ely area mines are a list of mine related deaths and a list of alternate names given for cross reference. The document source for each miner is shown by symbols next to his name and the key to the symbols is given at the end of the list.

Anne Stewart
Research Volunteer

#	Name	Nationality	Death Date	Newspaper Date	Mine	Comments	Age	
1 .	Aarjala, Otto	Finland	April 8, 1900	Ely Times, April 13, 1900	Pioneer	Death Record says Hamala	45	M
2	Anderson, Andrew	N/A	July 23, 1889	Iron Home, July 30, 1889	Chandler			S
3	Anderson, Matt	Finland	June 7, 1894	Ely Times, June 8, 1894	Chandler	Accident approximately 2 weeks prior	26	
4	Anderson, Otto	N/A	June 12, 1893	Ely Times, June 16, 1893	Chandler			
5 .	Antonelli, Mariano	Italy	Nov. 7, 1900	Ely Miner, Nov. 9, 1900	Chandler		38	
6 . *	Antonsich, Frank	Austria	Nov. 9, 1914	Ely Miner, Nov. 20, 1914	Sibley	Death Record says Antonsic	24	M
7 . *	Antonsich, Fred	Austria	Nov. 9, 1914	Ely Miner, Nov. 20, 1914	Sibley	Death Record says Ferdenano Antznic	41	M
8 . * +	Antonsich, John	Austria	Jan. 31, 1911	Ely Miner, Feb. 3, 1911	Pioneer	Two listed in MMD, but only one found in records	33	
9 x +	Arko, John	Austria	Mar. 27, 1918	Ely Miner, Mar. 29, 1918	Consolidated	Mud Creek. DR says Arke, + Record Perkay	42	M
10 *	Banks, Frank Jr.	USA, Ely	May 24, 1946	Ely Miner, May 30, 1946	Zenith	Motorman working on stockpile trestle		
11 +	Barich, John		Oct. 11, 1890	Missing issue of paper		Only record is the + Record.	47	M
12 . *	Beckstram, Leander	Sweden	Mar. 30, 1911	Ely Miner, April 7, 1911	Pioneer	Paper says Backstram, MMD Finn, d 3/20/1911	25	S
13 +	Belaj, Frank	Austria	Jan. 17, 1893	Ely Times, Jan. 20, 1893	Chandler		33	M
14 . */	Benzo, Guiseppe	Italy	Jan. 10, 1918	Ely Miner Jan. 18, 1918	Zenith		24	
15 x/	Bevic, Matt	Austria	Mar. 27, 1918	Ely Miner, Mar. 29, 1918	Consolidated	Mud Creek. Inspectors Report says Bevis	44	M
16 . +	Boiz, John	Austria	June 18, 1895	Ely Times, June 21, 1895	Chandler	Death Record says Bojc		
17 +	Bojc, John	Austria	Nov. 7, 1891	Ely Times, Nov. 13, 1891	Chandler	+ Record = Frank Bojec. d.11/10/91		
18	Boje, Frank	Austria	Oct. 29, 1890	Missing issue of paper	Chandler	No source for identification		
19	Bojec, Joseph		Dec. 5, 1892		Chandler	+ Record		
20	Bottish, Marcus	N/A	Oct. 29, 1890	Missing issue of paper	Chandler	No source for identification	32	M
21 . /*	Bridson, George	England	Mar. 17, 1920	Ely Miner, Mar. 19, 1920	Sibley	Inspectors Report says Brimson, age 34	28	
22 .	Caimi, Carlo	Italy	Jan. 8, 1920	Ely Miner, Jan. 9, 1920	Zenith	Miner says in occupation army, Germany	34	
23 .	Carlson, Nickelai	Finland	July 6, 1900	Ely Miner, July 6, 1900	Pioneer	Nickleai Juhntson on Death Record	52	M
24 *	Cencic, Vida	Jugoslavia	Nov 6, 1944	Ely Miner, Nov. 9, 1944	Pioneer	Mud slide	23	S
25 . *+	Chimgar, Frank	Austria	Feb. 20, 1907	Ely, Miner, Mar. 1, 1907	Zenith	+ Record says Chimzar	51	M
26 . *	Chistopher, John Peter	USA, Mich.	Feb. 16, 1922	Ely Miner, Feb. 24, 1922	Zenith	Age 50 in MMD	33	M
27	Colombo, Ferdinand	Italy	Sept. 20, 1899	Ely Times, Sept. 22, 1899	Pioneer			
28 .	Dianavic, Frank	Austria	May 2, 1903	Ely Miner, May 8, 1903	Pioneer	Given as name not known in paper	59	M
29 . */+	Drobnik, John	Austria	Dec. 10, 1924	Ely Miner, Dec. 12, 1924	Pioneer	MMD = 60. + Record says Drobinech	45	M
30 .	Elliot, E. B	N/A	June 21, 1899	Ely Times, June 23, 1899	Zenith			
31 . *	Erickson, John	Sweden	April 4, 1889	Iron Home, April 9, 1889	Chandler		30	S
32 .	Erickson, Victor	Finland	June 25, 1896	Ely Times, June 26, 1896	Pioneer		50	M
33 . *	Evonoff, Nick	Bulgaria	Oct.11, 1938	Ely Miner, Oct. 13, 1938	Sibley	Fell. Widow/son in Bulgaria. MMD=Evanoff	30	
34 . *	Floridan, George	Austria	Nov. 9, 1914	Ely Miner, Nov. 20, 1914	Sibley			M
35	Franske, Oscar			Ely Miner, Nov. 21, 1913	Mud Creek	Lived in Tower		

No.	Name	Country	Date	Newspaper	Location	Notes	Age	
36 *	Fusco, Emil	Italy	Feb. 2, 1927	Ely Miner, Feb. 4, 1927	Pioneer	MMD=Emanuelle Fisca, age 31)	30	
37 +	Geleznik, John	Austria	Jan. 11, 1903	Ely Miner, Jan. 16, 1903	Sibley	Paper says Zeleznik		
38 +	Gerbajs	Austria	Feb. 9, 1894	Ely Times, Feb. 9, 1894	Chandler	Paper gives no name.		S
39 .	Gerdovik, Geo	N/A	Nov. 8, 1901	Ely Miner, Nov. 8, 1901		Death Record says Gedosick	19	
40 *	Glinsek, Joseph Jr.	USA, Ely	Sept. 30, 1955	Ely Miner, Oct. 6, 1955	Pioneer	Cave in. MMD age = 43	42	M
41 .	Globinick, John	Austria	May 9, 1902	Ely Miner May 9, 1902	Pioneer		24	
42 x	Gorce, Matt	Austria	Oct. 12, 1909	Ely Miner, Oct. 15 1909	Sibley			
43 .	Gorse, Louis	Austria	April 16, 1910		Zenith	Death Rcrd.says Alvis Gorse. Cem. Record = Louis		
44 .	Gribbon, Chas	England	Mar. 20, 1896	Ely Times, Mar. 20, 1896	Chandler	Died while setting explosives. Death unexplained	36	M
45 .	Gustafson, Charles	Sweden	Nov. 9, 1899	Ely Times, Nov. 10, 1899	Bale's Camp	Exploration site near Robinson Lake		
46 .	Hakola, John	Finland	May 12, 1891	Ely Times, May 15, 1891	Chandler		22	
47 .	Hannan, Ole	N/A	June 19, 1889	Iron Home, June 25, 1889	Chandler			
48 *	Hanson, Louis		June 22, 1889		Chandler			
49 *	Hanula, Matt	Finland	June 13, 1889	Iron Home, June 18, 1889	Chandler	MMD = Nat Hanala	26	M
50 .	Haycock, George	Austria	June 25, 1896	Ely Times, June 26, 1896	Pioneer	Death Record says Hervok	39	M
51 *x/-	Heitalahti, Oscar	Finland	Mar. 24, 1924	Ely Miner Mar. 28, 1924	Pioneer	Remains to Michigan. Insp. Report=Hiltalathi	38	M
52 .	Hobich, Matt	Austria	July 9, 1903	Ely Miner, July 10, 1903	Savoy	Paper says John Habitch	32	M
53 */	Hubar, Josef	Austria	Aug. 9, 1913	Ely Miner, Aug. 15, 1913	Zenith	Inspector's Report says Hubat. MMD=d Aug. 8		
54 .	Hufta, Matt	Finland	Dec. 8, 1902	Ely Miner, Dec. 12, 1902	Pioneer	Death Record says Huhta	28	S
55 */	Humar, John	Austria	Nov. 9, 1914	Ely Miner, Nov. 20, 1914	Sibley	MMD & Inspt. Report=Homer	46	M
56 x	Indihar, Frank	N/A	Jan. 23, 1918	Ely Miner, Jan. 25, 1918	Section 30		35	
57 .	Ivic, Leopold	Austria	Jan. 10, 1900	Ely Times, Jan. 12, 1900	Chandler	or Inic. Wrongful death suit filed & dropped		
58 .	Jardi, Carl	Finland	July 15, 1918	Ely Miner, July 19, 1918	Section 30			
59	Jersin, Martin	Sweden	Dec. 22, 1895		Chandler	+ Record		
60 .	Johnson, Anton	Finland	Jan. 14, 1892	Ely Times, Jan. 15, 1892	Zenith		33	
61 .	Johnson, Herman	Bulgaria	Mar. 30, 1896	Ely Times, April 3, 1896	Pioneer		23	M
62 .	Johnson, Peter	Finland	June 30, 1917	Ely Miner, July 6, 1917	Section 30			
63 .	Jokela, Matt	Finland	Jan. 14, 1901	Ely Miner, Jan. 18, 1901	Pioneer			
64 .	Jylha, Jacob	Finland	March 20, 1904	Ely Miner, Mar. 25, 1904	Zenith			
65 .	Kajute, Erik	Finland	Oct. 24, 1900	Ely Miner, Oct. 26, 1900	Chandler		33	
66 *	Kangas, John	Finland	April 15, 1916	Ely Miner, April 21, 1916	So. Chandler	MMD = age 50	53	W
67 .	Kauppi, Jacob	Finland	Nov. 5, 1901	Ely Miner, Nov. 8, 1901	Pioneer		36	S
68 *	Klanfer, Luka	Jugoslavia	Sept. 20, 1948	Ely Miner, Sept. 23, 1948	Zenith	Ore fall. Wife in Yug. MMD = Luks Klanfar	59	M
69 *	Klobuchar, John	Finland	Dec. 10, 1942	Ely Times, Dec. 17, 1942	Chandler		45	M
70 .	Knous, John		Mar. 22, 1899	Ely Miner, Mar. 24, 1899	Chandler	Paper says Austrian	25	S
71 .	Koloski, John	Austria	Dec. 23, 1901	Ely Miner, Dec. 27, 1901	Pioneer	2 last names on Death Cert. Lahomacky	34	M

No.	Name	Birthplace	Death Date	Newspaper	Mine/Place	Notes	Age	Status
72 .	Konel, George	Austria	Oct. 14, 1899	Ely Miner, Oct. 20, 1899	Chandler	+ Record.	32	
73 +	Koren, Stephen		Sept. 11, 1890	Missing issue of paper				
74 .	Korvilla, Sakri	Finland	May 20, 1907	Ely Miner, May 24, 1907	Pioneer	Death Record says Gus Erickson	46	S
75 . *	Kosa, Joseph	Austria	April 28,1906	Ely Miner, May 4, 1906	Savoy	MMD also lists a Kotze, Sibley mine.	23	S
76 .	Kosier, John	Austria	July 8, 1901	Ely Miner, July 12, 1901	Savoy	Death Record says Kichenor	28	S
77 *+	John Kovach	Yugoslavia	June 4, 1937	Ely Miner, June 10, 1937	Pioneer		48	M
78 .	Kozeliever, Lorenz	Austria	April 4, 1901	Ely Miner, April 12, 1901	Savoy	Death Record says Lawrence		M
79 *+	Kramer, Anthony		June 4, 1937	Ely Miner, June 10, 1937	Pioneer	Cave in. + Record says Anton Kromar		M
80 .	Kramer, Frank	Austria	June 25, 1896	Ely Times, June 26, 1896	Pioneer	Paper says Cramer	27	S
81 +	Kreshman , Josph	Austria	Dec. 16, 1890	Iron Home, Dec. 23, 1890	Chandler	+ Record says Nosse		M
82	Kuhar, Frank	USA, Ely	Oct. 10, 1953	Ely Miner, Oct. 15, 1953	Pioneer	Blasting accident. WWII vet	37	M
83 . *	Kumppulainen, Ed	Finland	Jan. 8, 1918	Ely Miner, Jan. 18, 1918	So. Chandler	Death Record says Edmond Kumpalonen	44	M
84 .	Kunnari, Elias	Finland	April 21, 1903	Ely Miner, April 24, 1903	Zenith		28	M
85 .	Kure, Peter	Austria	May 17, 1895	Ely Times, May 17, 1895	Chandler		26	S
86 *+	Kuzma, Leopold	Austria	June 3, 1927		Sibley	+ Record says Kuzince		M
87 *	Latva, John	Finland	June 20, 1934	Ely Miner, June 22, 1934	Pioneer			M
88 . *	Lauritz, Stephen	Austria	Dec. 20, 1906	Ely Miner, Dec. 21, 1906	Sibley		24	
89 x	Lindbeck, John J.	N/A	Jan. 25, 1912	Ely Miner, Jan. 26 ,1912	Section 30			
90 .	Llias, Chas	Finland	Oct. 9, 1902	Ely Miner, Oct. 17, 1902	Chandler	Death Record has Leas	25	
91 .	Luoma, John	Finland	May 10, 1900	Ely Miner, May 11, 1900	Pioneer		22	
92 +	Luper, Joseph	Austria	Dec. 30, 1890	Ely Times, Jan. 2, 1891	Pioneer		24	
93 .*x	Lukavetz, Frank	Austria	Oct. 26, 1907	Ely Miner, Nov. 1, 1907	Pioneer	First wrongly identified as John Prishila		
94	Mackovitz, Paul	Austria	Dec. 7, 1902	Ely Miner, Dec. 11, 1902	Pioneer	MMD=Luzavich, Cemtry-Luzovech, + =Luzover		M
95 .	Magnuson, Nels	Sweden	Oct. 23, 1897	Ely Times, Oct. 29, 1897	Chandler	Paper says Muckovitz	38	M
96 +	Majerle, Juris	Austria	Nov. 14, 1889	Iron Home, Nov. 21, 1889	Chandler	Newspaper says George		
97 .+	Makauc, Paul	Austria	Dec. 9, 1895	Ely Times, Dec. 13, 1895	Pioneer	+ Record says Makavc	21	S
98 .	Maki, John		Feb. 21, 1892	Ely Times, Feb. 26, 1892	Chandler	Died in fire		
99	Maki, Matt	Finland	Date unknown	Ely Miner, Sept. 28, 1944	unknown	Died after long illness. Shock from a live wire		
100 .	Maki, Ralph E.	USA, Ely	March 7, 1960	Ely Miner, Mar. 10, 1960	Pioneer	Falling rock	49	M
101 .	Makie, Jack	Finland	Jan. 31, 1903	Ely Miner, Feb. 6, 1903	Pioneer	Death Record says Jacob Maki	33	M
102 . *	Malarich, Anton	Austr./Slov.	Jan. 27, 1921	Ely Miner, Jan. 28, 1921	Zenith	Death Record=Maslarich, MMD= Malaich, age 29	26	S
103 . *	Malich, John	Austria	Aug. 17, 1916	Ely Miner, Aug. 18, 1916	Zenith	Death Record=Maslarich, MMD= Malaich, age 29	30	S
104 . *	Manteggio, John	Italy	July 26, 1906	Ely Miner, July 27, 1906	Savoy		27	M
105 .*+	Martinen, August	Mexico	Aug. 9, 1918	Ely Miner, Aug. 16, 1918	Pioneer	Death Record=Martiner. MM =Martin age 35	33	S
106 .*x	Mattila, John	Finland	Mar. 27 , 1917	Ely Miner, Mar. 30, 1917	So. Chandler	Death Record says Mattala. MMD = d March 23	45	W
107 x	Matasic, George	Austria	Sep. 19, 1916	Ely Miner, Sept. 22, 1916	Semer	Consolidated Vermilion Mine	24	

No.	Name	Country	Date	Source	Location	Notes	M/S	Age
108 +	Mautz, Frank	Austria	June 6, 1894	Ely Times, June 8, 1894	Chandler	+ Record says Mauc		32
109 .	Mayanpa, Matt	Finland	May 3, 1905	Ely Miner, May 5, 1905	Pioneer			22
110 .	Mellund, Ole	Norway	Jan. 18, 1905	Ely Miner, Jan. 20, 1905	Zenith			25
111 ./	Mertel, Michael	Austria	April 22, 1913	Ely Miner, April 25, 1913	Pioneer	DR=Mikarl. A relative & Inspect. Rep.=Martel	M	29
112 *	Metsapelto, Henry	Finland	Feb. 12, 1942	Ely Miner, Feb. 19, 1942	Pioneer	Injured Nov. 9, 1941	M	61
113 +	Mihelich, John	Austria	June 28, 1893	Ely Times, June 30, 1893	Chandler	+ Record says George	M	50
114 *	Milkovich, Joseph	Jugo-Slavia	May 19, 1928	Ely Miner, May 25, 1928	Sibley	Electrocuted working steam shovel. MMD=Austr.	M	50
115 x	Miller, Oscar	N/A	Sept. 15, 1916	Ely Miner, Sept. 15, 1916	McComber		M	
116 .	Moisala, Sakris	Finland	Oct. 31, 1892	Ely Times, Nov. 4, 1892	Chandler			50
117 .	Mokovich, Matt	Austria	April 14, 1896	Ely Times, April 17, 1896	Chandler	Death Record says Mukovic	S	22
118 +	Moroni, Frank	Italy	Feb. 5, 1894	Ely Times, Feb. 9, 1894	Chandler	Church Record Feb. 6 date		30
119 .+	Morowitz, Peter	Austria	July 8, 1896	Ely Times, July 10, 1896	Pioneer	Death Record says Morvitz, + Record Moravitz	M	53
120 .	Morrelli, August	Italy	July 27, 1896	Ely Miner, July 31, 1896	Pioneer	Death Record says Augustino. Paper=age 46	M	45
121 *	Movrin, John	Yugoslavia	Jan. 20, 1948	Ely Miner, Jan. 22, 1948	Pioneer		M	
122 */	Mrak, Frank	Austria	Aug. 15, 1922	Ely Miner, Aug. 18, 1922	Pioneer	MMD = age 47	M	42
123 .	Muckovich, John	Slovenia	Sept. 14, 1901	Ely Miner, Sept. 20, 1901	Pioneer		S	23
124 .*	Muhvich, John	Austria	Sept. 6, 1913	Ely Miner, Sept. 12, 1913	Sibley	DR=Markovich, IR & MMD=Mukovich	M	44
125	Name not known	Austria	April 4, 1902		Savoy			
126 *	Nappa, Charles Sr.	Finland	July 21, 1927	Ely Miner, July 22, 1927	Pioneer		M	
127 *+	Nemitz, John	Austria	June 23, 1925	Ely Miner, June 26, 1925	Pioneer	DR=Nemec. MMD=d 6/22, +Record=Nemevetz	S	33
128 .	Nick, Tom	Bulgaria	Feb. 19, 1917	Ely Miner, Feb. 23, 1917	Section 30		S	
129 *	Niemi, Toivo	Finland	May 31, 1916	Ely Miner, June 2, 1916	Pioneer	DR=Timo Nieminen. MMD, Insp. Rprt=Tomi,	M	27
130 .*	Novak, Michael	Slovenia	Sept. 21, 1922	Ely Miner, Sept. 22, 1922	Pioneer	Death Record says Austrian. MMD says M	S	26
131 *	Ogreen, John	Sweden	Jan. 31, 1889	Iron Home, Feb. 5, 1889	Chandler	1st Death Reported Chandler. MMD=Ogren, d 2/1		
132 . *	Oinonen, Gideon	Finland	Nov. 9, 1914	Ely Miner, Nov. 20, 1914	Sibley	MMD = Oinanen	M	37
133 .*/	Ojala, Alex	Finland	Jan. 28, 1917	Ely Miner, Feb. 2, 1917	So. Chandler	MMD says 37	S	33
134 .*	Ollanketa, Heikki	Finland	Aug. 6, 1907	Ely Miner, Aug. 9, 1907	Pioneer	Death Record says Henry Ketto		43
135 .	Oman, Edward	Finland	Sept. 2, 1896	Ely Miner, Sept. 9, 1896	Chandler	Paper says Omen	S	21
136	Oppel, William H. Jr.	N/A	April 5, 1918	Ely Miner, April 5, 1918	Section 30			21
137 *x	Ordshkovich, John	Slavenia	April 27, 1911	Ely Miner, April 28, 1911	Zenith	DR=Oveskovich, MMD Creskovich, Cmtry Oreskovich	M	30
138 .	Oreskovich, Steve	European	Sept. 6, 1918	Ely Miner, Sept. 13, 1918	Section 30			32
139	Ornell, John	Finland		Iron Home, Oct. 15, 1889	Chandler			
140 *	Pahkama, John	Finland	Aug. 28, 1920	Ely Miner, Sept. 3, 1920	Zenith	MMD says age 31	M	30
141 .	Paksh, Anton	Austria	Aug. 10, 1902	Ely Miner, Aug. 15, 1902	Savoy			24
142 .	Palisic, John	Austria	Mar. 5, 1901	Ely Miner, Mar. 8, 1901	Chandler	Death Record says Paulisich		43
143 .	Pallan, Nick	Finland	Nov. 30, 1902		Pioneer			43

No. / Name	Country	Date	Source	Mine	Comments	Age	
144 + Peris, Mike	Finland	Sept. 3, 1893	Ely Times, Sept. 8, 1893	Chandler	Listed as name not known in paper.	49	S
145 * Peschel, Joe	USA, Ely	Jan. 8, 1945	Ely Miner, Jan. 11, 1945	Pioneer	Motor ran off trestle	42	M
146.+Petrich, Joseph	Austria	Aug. 10, 1920	Ely Miner, Aug. 13, 1920	Pioneer	Death Record says Petric. + Record says John	35	D
147 * Peuha, William	Finland	Sept. 18, 1930		Zenith			M
148 x/ Pietikaninen, Abraham	Finland	May 9, 1913	Ely Miner, May 16, 1913	Lucky Boy	Inspector's Report says Abram Pietikanien	41	
149 + Pietro, Tolero	Italy	Aug. 2, 1892	Ely Times, Aug. 5, 1892	Chandler		33	M
150 /+ Plahuta, Frank	Austria	Mar. 27, 1918	Ely Miner, Mar. 29, 1918	Consolidated	Mud Creek	52	M
151 + Plutz, John		Oct. 13, 1890	Iron Home, Oct. 14, 1890	Chandler	+ Record says body not found, paper says it was.		M
152 x Pogoreiz, Anton		May 10, 1913	Ely Miner, May 16, 1913	Section 30	Cemetery Record says Pogoretc		M
153 . Poost, John	Austria	Oct. 11, 1889	Iron Home, Oct. 15, 1889	Chandler			
154 . * Prejatelj, Anton		Mar. 13, 1906	Ely Miner, Mar. 16, 1906	Chandler	Andrew on Death Record	24	M
155 . Prijatelj, Frank	Austria	June 6, 1900	Ely Miner, June 8, 1900	Chandler	Frank Krijakly on Death Record	30	M
156 * Pusari, John		Oct. 15, 1956	Ely Miner, Oct. 18, 1956	Zenith			
157 . Quick, John	England	April 30, 1896	Ely Times, May 1, 1896	Zenith			
158 . Ranta, Mike		Nov. 15, 1913	Ely Miner, Nov. 21, 1913	Mud Creek			M
159 * Ranta, Otto	Finland	Nov. 14, 1947	Ely Miner, Nov. 20, 1947	Pioneer	Mud slide	56	M
160 . Renikka, John	Finland	Sept. 23, 1914	Ely Miner, Sept. 25, 1914	Section 30		24	S
161 . Rintimaki, John	Finland	Oct. 7, 1901	Ely Miner, Oct. 11, 1901	Chandler	Death Record says Rindamaki	36	S
162 * Robertson, Ernest	Canada	Sept. 6, 1946	Ely Miner, Sept. 12, 1946	Pioneer	Cave in	44	M
163 .+ Rock, Louis	Fr. Canada	June 17, 1922	Ely Miner, June 23, 1922	Pioneer			M
164 .*/Rom, Kasper	Austria	Jan. 4, 1918	Ely Miner, Jan. 4, 1918	No. Chandler	Inspector's Report says Casper. MMD=52	57	M
165 . Rova, Isaac	Finland	Dec. 20, 1898	Ely Times, Dec. 23, 1898	Pioneer	Paper says about age 32	29	M
166 * Rozman, George	Austria	July 19, 1930	Ely Miner, July 25, 1930	Sibley		45	M
167 *+Rus, John	N/A	Sept. 3, 1908	Ely Miner, Sept. 4, 1908	Pioneer	MMD = 30	40	M
168 . Salmi, Matti	Finland	April 2, 1903	Ely Miner April 3, 1903	Pioneer		24	M
169 . St. Claire, W. H.		Nov. 7, 1911	Ely Miner, Nov. 10, 1911	Section 30		30	M
170 x*Sankovitch, Joe	Austria	July 8, 1911	Ely Miner, July 14, 1911	Section 30		19	S
171 . Schustar, Anton	Austria	Aug. 12, 1903	Ely, Miner, Aug. 14, 1903	Savoy	Death Record=Scuster	29	
172.*+Selarovich, Vasar	Austria	Aug. 10, 1918	Ely Miner, Aug. 16, 1918	Pioneer	DR.=Vaso Severovich. MMD= Chandler	42	M
173 . Seraphine, Joseph Sr.		May 20, 1910	Ely Miner May 20, 1910		Died from injuries received in 1899		
174 * Silvola, Elmer	USA, Winton	Aug. 19, 1959	Ely Miner, Aug. 27, 1959	Zenith	Falling rock	41	M
175 * Simonich, John	Slovenia	April 8, 1930	Ely Miner, April 11, 1930	Sibley	Death Record says Simonitch	48	M
176 *+ Simonick, Mike	Austria	Dec. 14, 1902	Ely Miner, Dec. 19, 1902	Savoy			
177 .+ Sjonce, John	Austria	June 21, 1902	Ely Miner, June 27, 1902	Pioneer	Newspaper=Zgonc, Savoy mine. +Record=Zgonc		
178 . Sjostrom, Isaac	Finland	June 26, 1896	Ely Miner, July 1, 1896	Pioneer		33	M
179 . Skorich, Ignetz	Austria	Sept. 5, 1899	Ely Times, Oct. 13, 1899	Pioneer	Death Record says Glowich. Also in Ely Miner	24	S

#	Name	Origin	Date	Newspaper	Location	Notes	Age	M/S
180 *+	Skraba, John	Jugo-Slavia	Aug. 18, 1936	Ely Miner, Aug. 20, 1936	Zenith	Cable Snapped	53	M
181 . *	Skrejano, John	Slovenia	Sept. 6, 1910		Zenith		26	S
182 +	Slobodnick, Matt	Austria	Nov. 5, 1891	Ely Times, Nov. 6, 1891	Chandler		about 40	
183 .	Smrekar, Joseph	Austria	Feb. 5, 1900	Ely Miner, Feb. 9, 1900	Zenith		20	
184 .	Solumi, Elias	Finland	Nov. 20, 1901	Ely Miner, Nov. 22, 1901	Chandler	Death Record says Salmi	28	S
185 *	Steffens, Alden L	USA	June 14, 1952	Ely Miner, June 19, 1952	Zenith	Fall on June 6. MMD = d June 6	28	
186 .	Sterila, Matt	Austria	Aug. 16, 1901	Ely Miner, Aug. 16, 1901	Pioneer		32	S
187 .	Sterk, Peter	Austria	Aug. 3, 1903	Ely Miner, Aug. 6, 1903	Sibley		19	S
188 .	Sterlick, Rudolph	Austria	Dec. 6, 1902	Ely Miner, Dec. 12, 1902	Zenith			M
189 +	Sternot, Frank	Austria	Oct. 1, 1895	Ely Times, Oct. 4, 1895	Pioneer	Death Record. says Starnat, + Record Sternad + Record says Strucel	51	M
190 +	Strucklen, Matt	Slovenia	Jan. 7, 1902	Ely Miner, Jan. 10, 1902	Sibley		21	
191 *+	Stukel, Matt	Austria	Feb. 20, 1929	Ely Miner, Feb. 22, 1929	Pioneer	Crushed by fall of ore. +Record=Strukel	about 40	M
192 .	Stupetz, Ferdinand	Austria	May 10, 1902	Ely Miner, May 16, 1902	Sibley	Death Record says Stuptza	45	
193 .	Stustrom, Isaac	Finland	June 26, 1896	Ely Miner, July 1, 1896	Pioneer	DR says Sjastrom. Accident Rep. 6/26/1896		
194 .	Thomasin, Anton	Austria	May 8, 1895	Ely Times, May 10, 1895	Chandler	Death Record says Tomashin Jr.		S
195 .	Thumer, Alexander	Finland	Mar. 14, 1896	Ely Times, Mar. 20, 1896	Chandler	Death Record. says Tuamari		
196 .	Tikkanen	N/A	Jan. 17, 1915	Ely Miner, Jan. 22, 1915	Section 30			
197 . *	Tolenen, Sylvester	Finland	Jan. 19, 1908	Ely Miner, Jan. 24, 1908	Pioneer	Newspaper says Tolonenin	45	M
198 .	Tuoppala, Levi	Finland	June 14, 1903	Ely Miner June 19, 1903	Savoy	Death Record says Tuoppalla & Pioneer Mine	22	S
199 .	Unsijarvi, Sakris	Finland	Dec. 5, 1894	Ely Times Dec. 7, 1894	Chandler			
200 .	Verrant, John	Austria	July 30, 1901	Ely Miner, Aug. 2, 1901	Savoy	Newspaper=age 26	27	S
201 .	Vesil, Luke	Austria	Feb. 10, 1899	Ely Miner, Feb. 15, 1899	Pioneer	Newspaper = Lucas Vesel	36	M
202 . *	Vukelich, John	Slov/Austr.	Aug. 19, 1922	Ely Miner, Aug. 25, 1922	Zenith	MMD = d Aug. 18	36	M
203 . +	Vuksinic, John	Austria	July 10, 1902		Savoy		45	M
204 *	Walli, Arvo	USA, ND	Mar. 15, 1966	Ely Miner, Mar. 17, 1966	Pioneer	Fall of dirt	54	M
205 .	Warra, Peter	Finland	Aug. 8, 1903	Ely Miner, Aug. 14 1903	Pioneer		44	M
206 .	Westerholm, John	Finland	Mar. 19, 1900	Ely Miner, Mar. 23, 1900	Pioneer	Also in Ely Times	26	M
207 x	Wiiki, Wm.	Finland	Sept. 23, 1909	Ely Miner, Sept. 24, 1909	Zenith			
208 .	Wiljanen, William	Finland	Aug. 20, 1914	Ely Miner, Aug. 21, 1914	Section 30	Death Record says Viljoneu	25	
209 *	Witri, Emil	Finland	Dec. 6, 1926	Ely Miner, Dec. 10, 1926	Zenith		44	S
210 .	Yates, Ed		March 17, 1892	Ely Times, Mar. 18, 1892	Pioneer	St. Louis County Death Records		
211 .	Yerns, John	N/A	April 7, 1919	Ely Miner, April 11, 1919	Section 30			
212 *	Zgnoc, John		April 16, 1956	Ely Miner, April 19, 1956	Zenith			M
213 x/	Zoretic, Geo	Austria	Mar. 27, 1918	Ely Miner, Mar. 29, 1918	Consolidated	Mud Creek	22	
214 .	Zupancic, George	Croat/Austr.	Nov. 5, 1921	Ely Miner, Nov. 11, 1921	Pioneer	Death Record says Juraj. Buried in Gilbert	34	S
215 *	Zupec, Anton	Austria	Sept. 16, 1927	Ely Miner, Sept. 23, 1927	Pioneer	Fell 200 feet	37	M

	Name	See / Reference	Date	Place	Notes	Age	Sex
	Benko, Frank	See Banks					
	Creskovich, John	See Ordshkovich,		Zenith		30	M
	Erickson, Gus	See Korvilla					
	Fisca, Emanuelle	See Fusco					
.	Glowich, Ignatz	See Skorich	Sept. 5, 1899	Pioneer			
	Hamala	See Aarjala					
	Habitch, John	See Matt Hobich					
	Junston	See Carlson					
	Karjakly, Frank	See Prijatelj					
.	Kotze, Joe		April 28, 1906	Chandler			
*	Lahomacky	See Koloski, John		Sibley listed. Maybe duplicate of Kosa at Savoy		34	M
.	Lenovich, Vasa	See Selarovich		Pioneer		42	
+	Nosse, Joseph	See Kreshman		No. Chandler Croatia	Ely Miner, Aug. 16, 1918		
	Perkay, John	See Arko					
	Zeleznik, John	See Geleznik	June 10, 1903				
+	Zgonc, John	See Sjonce	June 21, 1902				

*	Luzavetz, Frank	Oct. 26, 1909	Erroneously listed by Green's Mining Deaths. Article referred to 1907 death.
	John Prishila		Paper identified as victim when actual victim was Joseph Luper.

	Name	Date	Origin	Newspaper Reference	Place	Notes	Age	Sex
*	Antonsich, John		Austria			Green lists 2 men same name, same day. No other record for this one	22	
.	Boic, Andrew	Aug. 12, 1902	Austria	Ely Miner		Death Record says mine accident, paper says fell down steps at home		
.	Brula, Matt	Sept. 4, 1965	USA, Tower	Ely Miner, Sept. 9, 1965		Minn Tac Construction site, Mt. Iron. Struck by rock	62	M
.	Buterac, Eli	Jan. 20, 1921	Yugoslavia	Friday, Jan. 28, 1921	Zenith	Died of heart trouble in Zenith	42	
.	Cardroff, Peter E.	Jan. 28, 1912				Not sure mine accident		
	Delach, Frank		USA	Ely Miner, Mar. 16, 1939	Pioneer	Collapsed at work	60	
	Fromhartz, Charlie	May 15, 1901	USA	May 17, 1901	Pioneer	Child: Fell down shaft while playing	12	
	Gardner, Art	Mar. 12, 1957	USA, Illinois	Ely Miner, Mar. 28, 1957	Soudan Mine		41	M
	Hagar, John	Not Available	N/A	Ely Times, Oct. 23, 1895	Oliver	John Staberg sued for damages, doesn't say Ely mine		
	Hall, William				Ely Miner, Dec. 5, 1930	Pioneer	Heart attack as prepared to go underground	54	M
	Hill, Arthur			Ely Miner, Feb. 12, 1942		Killed in Soudan Mine		
.	Jaskala, Harvey	Dec. 24, 1909				Pioneer—suicide		

	Name	Origin	Date	Source	Company/Notes	Notes	Age	
	Koski, Jalmer	USA, Ely	Dec. 3, 1964	Ely Miner, Dec. 10, 1964		Died on the way to work	63	M
	Kuhar, Laurence			Ely Miner, Jan. 11, 1935		Heart attack	56	W
	Lake, Jalmer	USA, Tower	Aug. 16, 1951	Aug. 23, 1951	Sibley	Oliver Mining Company. Heart Attack while at work	60	M
.	Markonich, Joe		Feb. 23 1914			DC only. Not sure a mine accident		
	Martinio, Joe	Italy	Nov. 20, 1895	Ely Miner, Nov. 27, 1895	Died in Minnesota Mine			
	Nauha, Matt		Feb. 3, 1959	Ely Miner, Feb. 5, 1959	Pioneer	Dropped dead at work	59	M
.	Pogzsenz		Aug. 30, 1908			Not sure a mine accident		
	Prishil, John	Austria	Dec. 30, 1890	Iron Home, Dec. 30, 1890		Wrongly identified. Joseph Luper the victim		
	Puzel, John			July 20, 1934	Oliver Mining	Died of heart attack	58	M
.	Rapson, Samuel					Died at night in Captain's Dry		
	Simoncoc, Stephen	Poland		Ely Miner, Oct. 31, 1902	Pioneer	Killed crossing tracks on way home	44	
.	Stark, Peter	Austria	June 14, 1900	Ely Miner, June 22, 1900	Killed in Biwabik		34	
*/	Stupica, Leopold	Austria	Jan. 19, 1922			Murdered	38	S
	Takavitz, Tony	USA, Ely	May 27, 1955	Ely Miner, June 2, 1955		Doesn't say if a miner		
	Tekautz, Frank	USA, Soudan	Dec. 1, 1964	Ely Miner, Dec. 10, 1964	Pioneer	Died suddenly at work	61	M
x	Tome, Frank		Oct. 28, 1917	Ely Miner, Nov. 2, 1917	Killed in mine in Aurora			
	Trenbath, Sam	England	Oct. 14, 1895	Ely Miner, Oct. 16, 1895		"Paralysis of the heart"	35	
*	Yeskila, Henry	Finland	Dec. 26, 1909	Ely Miner, Dec. 31, 1909	Pioneer	Suicide. Looks like threw himself down mine shaft		
*	Zuponsic, Frank		Nov. 13, 1915		Pioneer	MMD says accident/ not death		M

/ = St. Louis County Inspector of Mines Annual Report May 1912 - December 1924

x = Cemetery Card

. = Death Record

* = Green list of Minnesota Mining deaths 1889-1990 (MMD)

+ = St. Anthony Church records

FOR FURTHER READING & RESEARCH...

Centennial Roaring Stoney Days (1958)

Eight Miles Without a Pothole – by Jim Klobuchar (1986)

Ely Since 1888 – The Ely Echo (1988)

Ely's West End – by Milton Stenlund (2002)

Ely-Winton Historical Society census and newspaper microfilm archives

Ely-Winton Historical Society picture archive collection

The End of the Road Reader II - by Hokkanen and Stewart (2000)

A History of Incredible Ely – by Lee Brownell (1976)

Growing Up in Ely – by Margaret Osaben Rawland (2005)

Lee Brownell picture collection (Ely-Winton Historical Society)

Pioneer Life in Ely – by Lee Brownell (1981)

Stories of Old Ely by Michael Hillman (2005)

The Zest and the Best of Klobuchar – by Jim Klobuchar (1967)

Where in the World is Calumet? - by David Kess (2008)

Yes, Really It's Ely – by Ruth King (1942 and reprinted in 2001)

*All publications available at the Ely Public Library and the Ely-Winton Historical Society. Most are also available for purchase at the
Ely-Winton Historical Society
Vermilion Community College
1900 E. Camp Street
Ely, MN 55731
phone ~ 218 – 365 – 3928
email ~ ewhs@vcc.edu

Additional copies of this book can also be purchased at the address above.

INDEX

NOTE: The Appendix of mining deaths has not been indexed. The names are alphabetized within the list.

ABOUT THE AUTHOR

David Kess is a third generation Elyite. Prior to his involvement with the Ely-Winton Historical Society he was a mathematics and history teacher in Aurora, MN, for thirty-four years.

At the historical society he compiled a booklet about mining locations in Ely entitled "Where in the World is Calumet" and was actively involved with editing the memoir of Simon Bourgin, an Ely native and a noted international journalist. He arranges exhibits and writes newspaper articles on local history. He writes for Finnish-American and dog breed publications.

Senja Maki was his grandmother and mentor for local history. She lived in Ely to age of 100 and was long active in local affairs. David now lives in the home his grandparents built in 1914.

This picture shows Chapman St. on the left and the schools on Harvey St. on the right. Since the Memorial High School is not shown, it was taken prior to 1924.

ABOUT THE FRONT COVER PHOTO...

From 1888 on the railroad was the lifeline to and from Ely. It transported ore, freight, and passengers out of town and brought waves of new immigrant families to Ely. Jewish families here got kosher meat from Duluth sent by rail. Often it was spoiled and the families were left without that option. The railroad extended to Winton three miles further and originally also brought out the lumber from the St. Croix and Swallow Hopkins sawmills there. Riding to and from Winton for 15¢ was a treat children were occasionally given. The children in the photo are awaiting the arrival of the train to do that, to meet someone arriving, or just to see the train itself coming in.

Mining officials and mine fee holders often came from Duluth and the Iron Range to do business at the mining offices. The railroad was owned by the mining company and was called the Duluth, Mesabi, and Iron Range Railway. They also operated the telephone service for many decades until it was sold to Gopher State Telephone Company in 1962. Many seniors in town remember well the days of picking up a phone receiver and being asked, "Number please," by a local telephone operator at the Ely switchboard upstairs of the depot.

A year after the mines closed and US Steel sold the mining properties, including the railroad, the tracks were pulled out. The depot went vacant for awhile but later became the home of Wilderness Outfitters, a canoe trip outfitting and planning business. Its unique roofline still identifies it as a former railroad depot. The adjoining roundhouse became a heavy equipment storage facility for a local road construction firm.

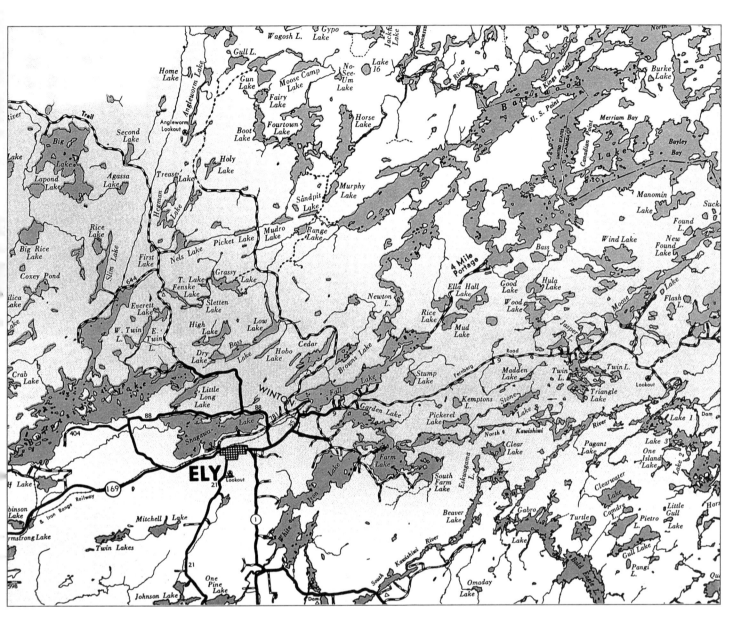

Ely sits in squarely in the middle of a nearly countless number of lakes and borders the million-acre Boundary Water Canoe Area. Nearly all the lakes are of glacial origin. Although it is only nine miles to the Canadian border "as the crow flies" to get there by road, one must travel either northwest to International Falls (102 miles) or northeast to Lake Superior and Pigeon River (and on to Thunder Bay, Ontario, 211 miles).

Courtesy of the Ely Chamber of Commerce and the W A Fisher Co., Virginia, MN